Understanding Weather

Understanding Weather

REVISED EDITION

HARRY MILGROM
Director of Science
New York City Public Schools

ILLUSTRATED BY LLOYD BIRMINGHAM

CROWELL-COLLIER PRESS
COLLIER-MACMILLAN LIMITED, LONDON

Library of Congress Catalog Card Number: 77–97756

The Macmillan Company
866 Third Avenue
New York, New York 10022

Collier-Macmillan Canada Ltd., Toronto, Ontario

Printed in the United States of America

First Printing

To Parents:

Through the advancement of science
your children will inherit a better world—
a world in which reason will triumph, and
peace will set the stage for all to enjoy
the fruits of man's genius

contents

U.S. DEPARTMENT OF COMMERCE
ENVIRONMENTAL SCIENCE SERVICES ADMINISTRATION
WEATHER BUREAU
SILVER SPRING, MD. 20910

Dear Reader,

I believe that most young people are more weather conscious than adults. Weather is often your closest contact with nature. You see evidence of its force—big, awesome and uncontrollable. Weather affects your daily activities and even the clothes you wear. You can appreciate that it's important to understand the weather. You want to know what is happening, what will happen next and why.

Weather is important to all countries of the world. In nearly every country, people measure the pressure, temperature, moisture and movement of air. Different countries exchange their reports and even help each other in making forecasts. They work together in the adventure of learning about the weather.

Harry Milgrom is one of the foremost interpreters of science for young people. He has written *Understanding Weather,* an outstanding book for all those who want to learn about the weather. It will be an excellent start for you as you begin to study this fascinating subject. I hope you will become so interested that you will want to continue learning about the weather all your life.

Sincerely yours,

George P. Cressman

GEORGE P. CRESSMAN
Director, Weather Bureau

Understanding Weather

1. Weather as You Like It

At some future time, if you are asked what you do for a living, you may be able to hand the person your business card. It may look like this:

> *The weather you want—made to order for all occasions*
>
> **WEATHER INCORPORATED**
>
> *E. Z. Wonders*
> *75 Windy Lane*
> *SUnshine 7-1212* *Anytown, U.S.A.*

Let us take an imaginary trip into the future and see how you operate your business.

Actually, you will work for the government because it must approve all requests that are sent to you. It would never do to let you or anyone else control the weather for personal gain. Too many people want opposite kinds of weather. But some special control of the weather may be in the public interest, such as creating fair weather on Election Day to give everyone a chance to vote.

You will make use of the weather reports of the Weather Bureau and of the space station satellites. Your chief tool will be good information. You will be able to know two weeks in advance what kinds of weather are on the way. Then you will act accordingly. Using high-energy rays, you will be able to remove the charges of thunder-clouds before they can cause an electrical storm. If rain is needed, you will know just when and where to send up airplanes to seed the clouds.

Some of your customers are listed below. The services requested show how important the weather is for many people.

ORGANIZATION	WEATHER REQUESTED
Nonpartisan Voters League	Sunny and mild on Election Day
U.S. Air Force Satellite Project	Calm wind and clear sky in Florida
Citrus Fruit Growers, Inc.	Temperatures not lower than 35° F.
Olympic Games Committee	Fair and seasonably warm during games
Operation Moonwatch	Cloudless skies after rocket launching
Dry Acres Planters, Inc.	Light but steady rainfall

It is easy to see that if you could really offer this kind of weather service, the whole world would beat a path to your door.

Why do people want to know about and control the weather? The answer is quite simple. Almost everything we have, eat, wear or do is affected in one way or another by the weather. All of us would like to be able to make our own weather or at least to know in advance what it is going to be.

Consider how important the weather is in your own life. Rainy weather may mean that you and your class cannot go on an outing or field trip that has been planned. Good weather may mean that a field day or kite-flying contest will be held as scheduled. Your activities change with the weather. A broiling sun sends you scurrying to the nearest pool or beach. A thunderstorm drives you indoors to play games or to read a book.

When you get up in the morning you look out the window to see what kind of day it is. It looks cloudy and you think perhaps it will rain. But you hate to wear boots or carry an umbrella—so what will you do? You will tune in the weather report on your radio or television. If a report is not available you can telephone for weather information or look at the weather forecast in the morning newspaper. Some boys and girls keep their own records to help them figure out what the weather is likely to be.

One of the most famous sayings about the weather is, "Everybody talks about the weather, but nobody does anything about it." Perhaps you will not agree after we take a tour around your house. If your house is like many modern houses, it has a fine variety of weather-making machines in it. Do you want to have "rain"? All you have to do is turn on a faucet. With just a twist of your wrist, you can make any kind of rain—from a gentle sprinkle to a drenching downpour—come from the showerhead in your bathroom. If you forget to turn off the water, your floors may be covered with a "flood."

Some buildings have sprinkler systems, which are always ready to put out a fire if one starts. It would be nice

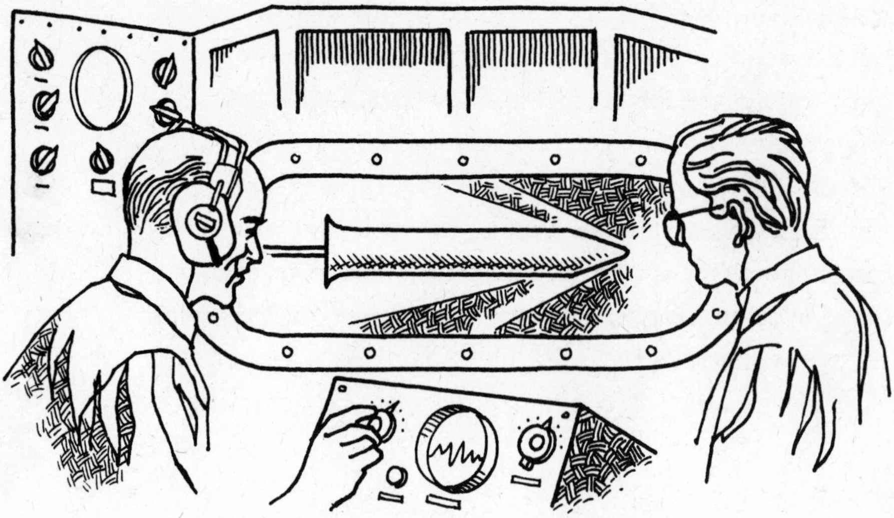

ROCKET PARTS
ARE TESTED
IN WIND TUNNELS

to have such protection for our forests. In the future, if you are a weathermaker, you may be called upon to wet down a dry forest *before* it catches fire.

Many buildings now have air-conditioning equipment for cooling the air. To make a "wind" indoors, all you have to do is switch on an electric fan. Depending upon the size and speed of the fan you can produce any kind of wind from a gentle breeze to a full gale. Many of the storm scenes you see in the movies are made to look real with the help of giant fans. Even airplane and rocket parts are tested in wind tunnels to see how they will stand up in flight.

Are the days too short or the nights too long? Whichever way you look at it, you have electric lamps to fill a room with homemade "sunlight."

What else besides homemade sunlight, rain and wind do you need to give you complete control of indoor weather? Can you do anything to regulate the temperature? Of course you can. When the outdoor weather is cold, you can turn on the heating system to pump heat into the house. When the air outside the house is too warm you can turn on the air cooler to pump heat out of the house. In either case, if you are too busy to keep track of the temperature yourself, a *thermostat* (*ther*-muh-stat) can control the temperature. A thermostat is a device to turn on or shut off a heating or cooling system at any temperature you select in advance.

In some modern homes and office buildings the windows can remain closed all year long. These buildings are fully air-conditioned. A complete air conditioner will do the following:

1. Heat or cool the air to suit your comfort.
2. Add moisture to the air if it is too dry.
3. Remove moisture from the air if it is too humid.
4. Circulate the air at various speeds.
5. Filter the dust and fumes from the air.

To be able to live and work in buildings that provide comfortable indoor weather is delightful. But delight is not the only reason for our wanting to control indoor weather. Sometimes it is an absolute necessity. Here are some examples. In hospitals the nursery and the operating rooms have to have the right conditions as a safeguard to health. People who raise chickens keep the eggs in an air conditioner called an incubator. The newborn chicks are kept in another type of unit called a brooder. In many laboratories where plants and animals are raised, the weather is controlled to provide the conditions needed for the experiment. In certain factories the atmosphere is weather-conditioned to protect the materials. The people who work in such plants may have to wear special clothing to protect themselves.

At this point you may be saying to yourself, "It does not seem to be too hard to make indoor weather. Is it possible to use similar methods to change weather conditions out in the open?" Here are the facts. You decide the answer.

Suppose the people in your town like to go ice skating as early in the fall and as late in the spring as possible. They may build an outdoor skating rink. In the process of construction, refrigerator coils are buried in the ground. To prepare the rink for skating, the surface is flooded with one or two inches of water, and the refrigerator system is turned on. In a few hours, the water freezes and the rink is covered with a layer of ice. Then in the fall and spring, even though the temperature of the air is above freezing (32° F.), the skaters glide around merrily on the little island of man-made winter.

Here is another example of how man can change outdoor weather. The Weather Bureau discovers that freezing temperatures are coming to Florida or California. What may happen if freezing temperatures come to those states? The lemons, oranges and grapefruit growing there may be ruined. Something must be done fast to raise the temperature of the air surrounding these trees a few degrees. In the spaces between the rows of trees, at intervals of about 15 feet, the fruit growers set up small, long-stacked iron stoves called smudge pots. Each stove is filled with crude oil or coke. When these fuels burn they give off a thick black smoke. The smoke from all the pots soon covers the entire orchard with a heavy blanket. By trapping the earth's heat under the smoke, the grove is made into a little island of warmth in an ocean of frost, and the crops are saved.

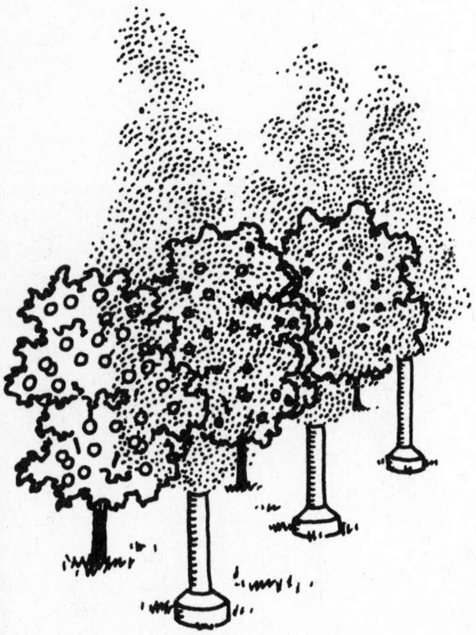

Another example is one you may find on superhighways. These roads are built so cars can travel on them at sixty or more miles per hour. That is fine as long as the drivers can see the road clearly, but sometimes fog covers a stretch of the road and slows traffic. Highway engineers have found a simple answer—blow the fog away. To do this they mount big electric fans on posts beside the road, and when the fog comes the fans are turned on. The man-made wind blows the fog right off the road and clears the path for the fast-moving cars.

Then there is the situation in which too much wind blows in certain places. Can anything be done about that? Wind cannot be stopped from blowing, but trees can be planted in its path. In any one region, winds usually blow from the same direction. Belts of trees planted across the path of winds break up their force. Without such wind breaks, some areas of our country—such as the Dust Bowl region—would soon become wasteland and desert.

You may be surprised to learn that sometimes there is not enough bad weather. You might call rainy weather "bad" because it prevents you from having certain kinds of outdoor fun. But a city or town or even you, may suffer if the weather is so "good" that no rain falls for a long period of time. Then the people look for ways to make rain fall. One of the ways of making rain fall is called *cloud seeding*. This can be done either from the ground or from airplanes. The idea is simple. Raindrops need something to cling to as they form. Dry ice and silver iodide are two materials that serve the purpose nicely. All you have to do is spread these materials around where there are clouds from which rain can fall. This gives the raindrops a chance to start forming.

Perhaps you see now that something can be done and often *is* done about the weather. You need not be a scientist to join this effort. All it takes is a bit of real interest and some ability to follow the guidelines that scientists are able to give you. As you read this book, you will discover some things about the weather that will help make it work *for* you, rather than against you.

You may even decide that you would like to become a weather forecaster or a weather "modifier." We do not expect you to become a real weather expert without years of devoted study, but you can get started *right now*.

2. The Earth and Sun—the Weather Team

The next time you are tempted to complain about the weather, asking, as people often ask, "What makes this weather so bad?" put the blame where it belongs. Energy from the sun, the earth, water and air act upon each other to make the weather.

Take the matter of changes in temperature. You probably have had plenty of experiences with the heating effects of the sun. For example, did you ever step quickly from deep shade into bright sunlight or from bright sunlight back into deep shade? In the first case you feel a sudden flash of warmth. In the second case you suddenly feel cooler. If you live in a city, you surely have noticed how people tend to walk on the sunny side of the street in the wintertime and on the shady side in summer.

When you experiment with sunlight or set up a home weather station, remember to put your thermometer in the shade. Professional weathermen always do this. In fact they use a shady shelter that is similar to the one shown in the picture, as a place in which to keep their thermometers and other instruments.

Do you notice something else about that shelter? It is well ventilated. The sides are not solid. Instead they have slits as openings for the air to enter and leave. There is a special reason for this. If you have ever put your head inside an automobile that has been parked for a time in the sunlight with the windows closed, you know the reason. It feels as if you had put your head into an oven.

Of course, there is a good scientific explanation for this. The rays of sunlight go through the glass windows of the car quite easily. Once inside the car, these rays are absorbed by the seats, leather and other materials, which then become hot. The heated objects give off energy but this cannot get out through the glass windows as easily as the sunlight entered. As a result the temperature inside the car rises higher and higher. Because the same thing happens in an all-glass greenhouse, scientists call it the *greenhouse effect*.

The greenhouse effect works not only with greenhouses and closed-up automobiles but also with the entire earth. This earth of ours is a planet with a protective blanket of gases, called the *atmosphere,* wrapped around it. The sun's light rays have little trouble passing through the atmosphere, but heat energy cannot leave as easily. Thus, the surface of the earth on which we live is warmed as if it were in a large greenhouse.

The lowest temperature ever recorded on earth was at Station Vostok near the South Pole. There a temperature of 125.3° F. below zero was recorded on August 24, 1960. On that same day thermometers at Cow Creek in Death Valley, California, showed a temperature of 105° F. above zero. This range of 230.3 degrees would be much greater if we had no atmosphere surrounding the earth like a protective blanket.

Extremes of Weather Conditions in the United States

Weather condition	To what extreme?	Where?	When?
BLIZZARD	One of the biggest: 21 inches of snow	Eastern U.S.A.	March 12–14, 1888
CLOUDBURST	One of the biggest: 12 inches of rain in 42 minutes	Holt, Missouri	June 22, 1947
CLOUDINESS	Least: 3/10 cover	Arizona	Average Yearly
	Most: 7/10 cover	Washington	Average Yearly
DEW	Most in one year: 10 inches	Coshocton, Ohio	Not Recorded
	Most in one night: 7/100 inch	Coshocton, Ohio	Not Recorded
DROUGHT	Very bad	In the Dust Bowl, which includes parts of Colorado, Kansas, Nebraska, New Mexico, Oklahoma, South Dakota, Texas and Wyoming	1950 to 1956
DUST STORMS	Severe	Same states as for drought	April, 1955
FLOOD	Very bad: 2,200 people drowned	Johnstown, Pennsylvania	May 31, 1889
FOG	Most	Los Angeles, California	Average Yearly
HAILSTONES	Largest: 5½ inches in diameter; 1½ pounds in weight	Potter, Nebraska	July 6, 1928
HURRICANE	One of the biggest: 650 people killed; $500,000,000 damage	Eastern U.S.A.: Long Island to New England	September 21, 1938
PRESSURE	Lowest: 26.35 inches	Craig, Long Key, Florida	September 2, 1935
	Highest: 31.40 inches	Helena, Montana	January 9, 1962
RAINFALL	Driest state: 9 inches per year	Nevada	Average Yearly
	Wettest state: 55 inches per year	Louisiana	Average Yearly
	Driest spot:1.6 inches per year	Death Valley, California	Average Yearly
	Wettest spot in 48 continental states: 144.43 inches	Wynoochee Oxbow, Washington	Average Yearly
	Biggest 24-hour rain: 38.7 inches	Yankeetown, Florida	September 5–6, 1950
	Biggest in 50 states: 460 inches	Mt. Waialeale, Island of Kauai, Hawaii	Average Yearly
SMOG	One of the worst: 20 people died	Donora, Pennsylvania	October 27, 1948
SNOW	Biggest snowflakes: 2½ inches	Topeka, Kansas	December 25–29, 1959
	Biggest single snowfall in 24 hours: 75.8 inches	Silver Lake, Colorado	April 14–15, 1921
	Biggest snowfall for one week: 141 inches	Ruby, Colorado	March 23–30, 1899
	Biggest snowfall for entire winter: 1,000 inches	Rainier Park, Washington	Winter of 1955–56
	Region of perpetual snow	Rocky Mountains	All Year
TEMPERATURE	Lowest: −70 ° below zero	Rogers Pass, Montana	January 20, 1954
	Highest: 134 °	Death Valley, California	July 10, 1913
THUNDERSTORMS	Most: About 100 per year	Lakeland, Florida	Average Yearly
TORNADO	One of the worst: 689 people killed; $16,000,000 damage	Missouri, Illinois and Indiana	1925
WIND	Highest speed: 231 miles per hour	Mt. Washington, New Hampshire	Not Recorded

On the moon, which has no atmosphere, the temperature ranges from a high of about 212° F. (the boiling point of water) at midday to a low of about 243° F. below zero at lunar midnight. On the moon this change of approximately 455 degrees takes place in about two weeks. That is the length of time between noon and midnight on the moon.

Thus, the earth's atmosphere not only helps the earth to hold much of its heat at night and during the winter but also protects the earth from the sun's rays. You may see for yourself how this greenhouse effect works on a small scale by placing a thermometer in a closed plastic bag in the sunlight. Compare the readings on this thermometer with those on a thermometer outside the bag. The temperature inside the bag may be 10–30 degrees higher.

Now let us investigate another weather mystery. You may have noticed when walking barefoot outdoors that some places on the ground were very hot while others were cooler. There is a good scientific reason for this. Let's find out by doing a simple experiment.

All you need for this experiment is a watch, a dish, some dark-colored soil, some light-colored sand and a thermometer.

First, put a cupful of dark-colored soil into the dish. Be sure the dish is in a shaded place where the temperature is about that of a normal room. Now put the bulb of the thermometer one-half inch below the surface of the soil. Read the temperature of the soil at once and make a record of it. Allow the soil and the thermometer to stay as they are for five minutes and record the temperature again. Take another reading five minutes later to be sure there is no further change. Now you are ready to put the whole setup into the direct rays of the sun. Again make a record of the temperature every five minutes until there is no further change. When you are through, go over the

DARK SOIL

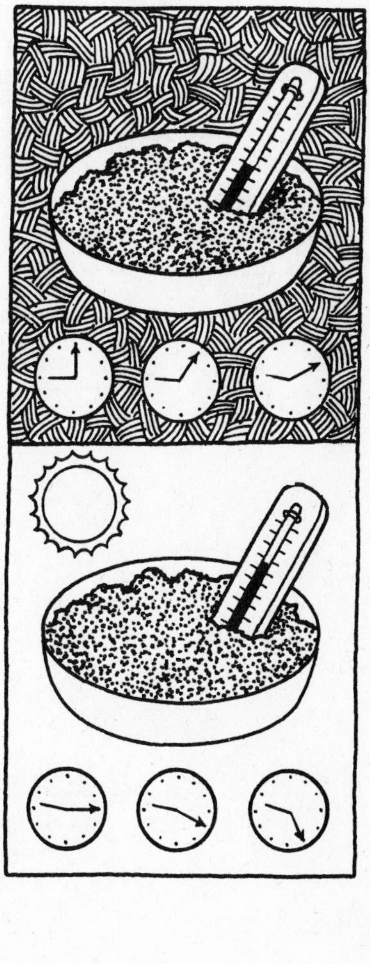

LIGHT SAND

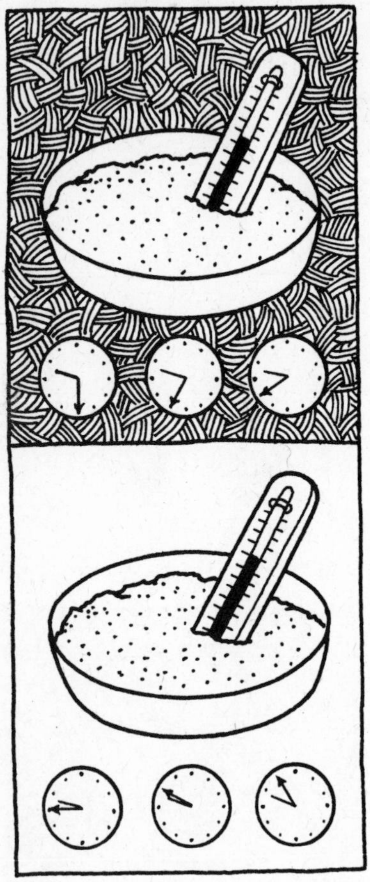

steps again using the same dish and the same thermometer—but now use the light-colored sand instead of the dark-colored soil.

Now compare your results with these.

	Time	Temperature
DARK SOIL IN SHADE	9:00	68° F.
	9:05	68° F.
	9:10	68° F.
DARK SOIL IN SUNLIGHT	9:15	72° F.
	9:20	74° F.
	9:25	76° F.

	Time	Temperature
LIGHT SAND IN SHADE	9:30	68° F.
	9:35	68° F.
	9:40	68° F.
LIGHT SAND IN SUNLIGHT	9:45	69° F.
	9:50	70° F.
	9:55	71° F.

In your experiment, did the soil temperature and the sand temperature rise when the dish was placed in the light? You probably expected this to happen, because the sun's rays warm things. But did you notice that the dark soil got hotter than the sand? The explanation is found in a well-known scientific principle that dark materials absorb the sun's energy better than light-colored materials, but they do not reflect it as well.

You can check this by covering the bulb of the thermometer with other types of light and dark materials, each having the same thickness. You will find it interesting to compare coverings of white cloth and black cloth or white paper and black paper of the same type. Even paints can be used. You will be able to think of other dark and light things to compare in the same way. When you are satisfied with your results, try another comparison. This time, place the thermometer bulb beneath the surface of a cupful of water that has been put into the dish. Go over the same steps as before. Keep the water in the shade until it reaches a temperature of 68° F. Then expose the water to sunlight and record its temperature every five minutes for ten or fifteen minutes. What happens? You will find that the temperature rises less in water than in either dish of soil. There are two good reasons for this. First, the surface of the water reflects light better than soil, and, second, more energy is needed to heat water.

Now you have to think big. In the previous experiments you used only a cupful of soil or water spread out in a dish. Think of large areas of the earth's surface—a lake, an ocean, a desert, a plowed field, a forest, a mountainside or a snow-covered field. Each of these will be warmed to different degrees by the rays of the sun. Each will warm the air above it differently. Each will be a factor in bringing on the weather changes you will learn about later.

Before we go into the story of these weather changes, we must look again at the earth as a planet receiving the sun's rays. If you have traveled north or south, you probably know that even a few hundred miles may cause weather differences. In many states, winters are colder in the north country than they are farther south. In summer, people who like cooler weather travel up into Maine and Canada. In winter, a great many people who like warmer weather travel to Florida or to southern California. Why should a few hundred or thousand miles make such a noticeable and enjoyable difference?

To find the answer, look at a globe. The earth may not be a perfect example of a globe, but the comparison is good enough for our purpose. The curve of the earth's surface is the thing to keep in mind. Do you suppose the curve of the earth has any effect upon the way the earth's surface is heated by the sun's rays? Can you explain why?

To answer this question, we will again experiment with a model that represents a part of the earth. The earth itself is so big that from where you are standing you cannot notice the curve in its surface. So make a surface with a curve you can see. Tack a strip of cardboard 22″ long to a strip of wood 11″ long. The width is not important; make it four or five inches. If you do not have these things handy, you can get them later. The drawing below shows you what the model looks like, so that you can understand what we are going to do.

We have mounted the curved section on a stand in a way that permits us to move the section. Fasten your thermometer first at line 1, then at line 2 and then at line 3. In each case, keep the model in full sunlight as shown. The thermometer bulb is covered with a piece of black paper or adhesive tape painted black, so as to soak up sunlight quickly. As a result, the temperatures change enough to show different readings clearly. This is what we found:

Thermometer on line	Starting temperature	Temperature after 2 minutes	Change in temperature
1	70° F.	82° F.	Up 12° F.
2	62° F.	70° F.	Up 8° F.
3	60° F.	62° F.	Up 2° F.

Where the sun's rays fall directly on a place, its temperature rises most. Where the sun's rays simply graze a place, its temperature rises least.

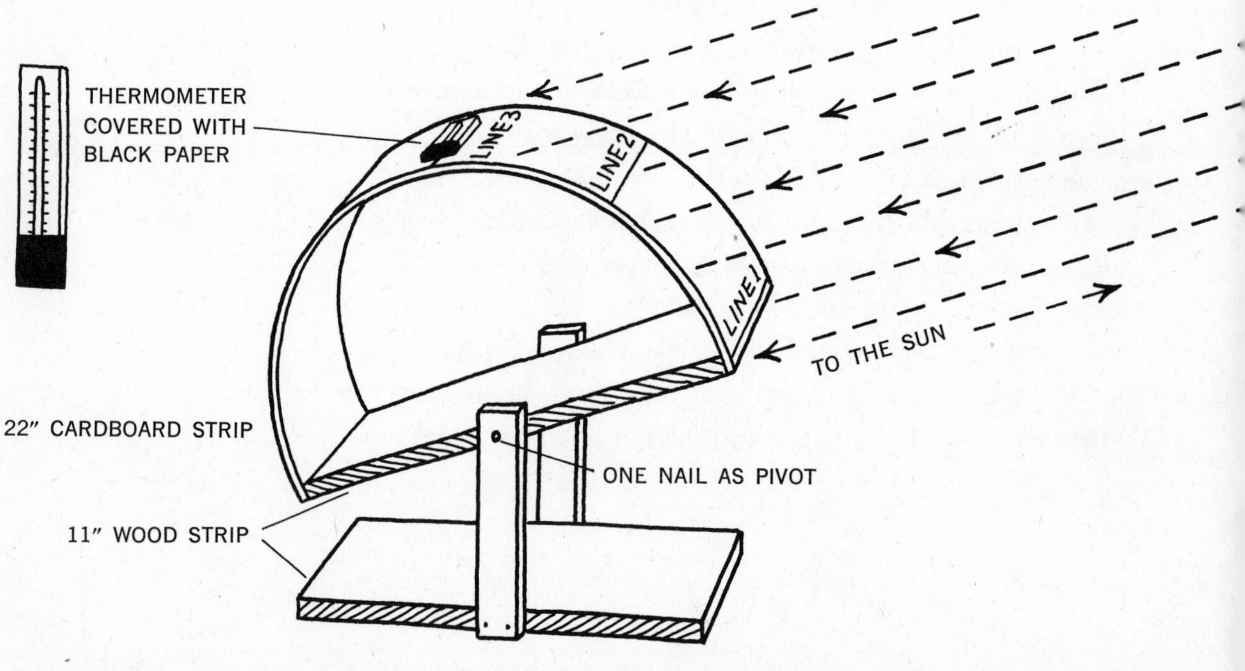

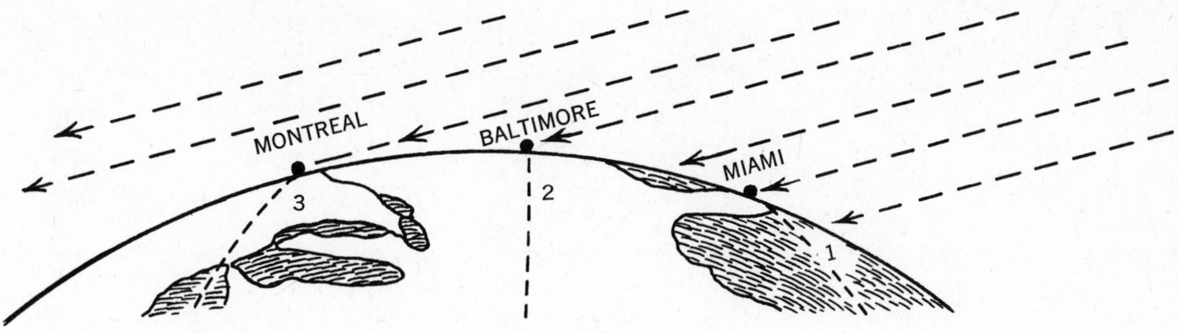

Where does anything like this happen on the surface of the earth? You will find the answer by looking at the drawing above. See how its shape resembles our curved piece of cardboard, but now you are looking at a drawing of a portion of the earth's curved surface. The city in the position matching line 3 is Montreal. The city in the position matching line 2 is Baltimore. The city in the position matching line 1 is Miami. With the sun in the position shown and *other things being the same,* Miami thermometers will show a higher temperature than those in Baltimore. Baltimore's will read higher than the thermometers in Montreal.

One important thing to remember is expressed in those five little words "other things being the same." The "other things" include a great many conditions that may vary from place to place. In one, rain may be falling from clouds that blot out the sun's rays. In another, a fog may hide the sun's rays. In the third, the day may be clear and bright. For the kind of scientific observations needed, we have to rely on the Weather Bureau which does the job several times a day, year after year.

What you have learned about one type of weather change in the region of the earth's surface called the United States is a clue to the story of weather changes anywhere in the world, from North Pole to South Pole. Because of its curved surface, the earth has five great temperature zones ranging from the hot one around the equator to the cold ones near the poles. These are shown in the diagram. Do you see the names of the boundaries of these zones? If you do not know them, you may wish to learn them now.

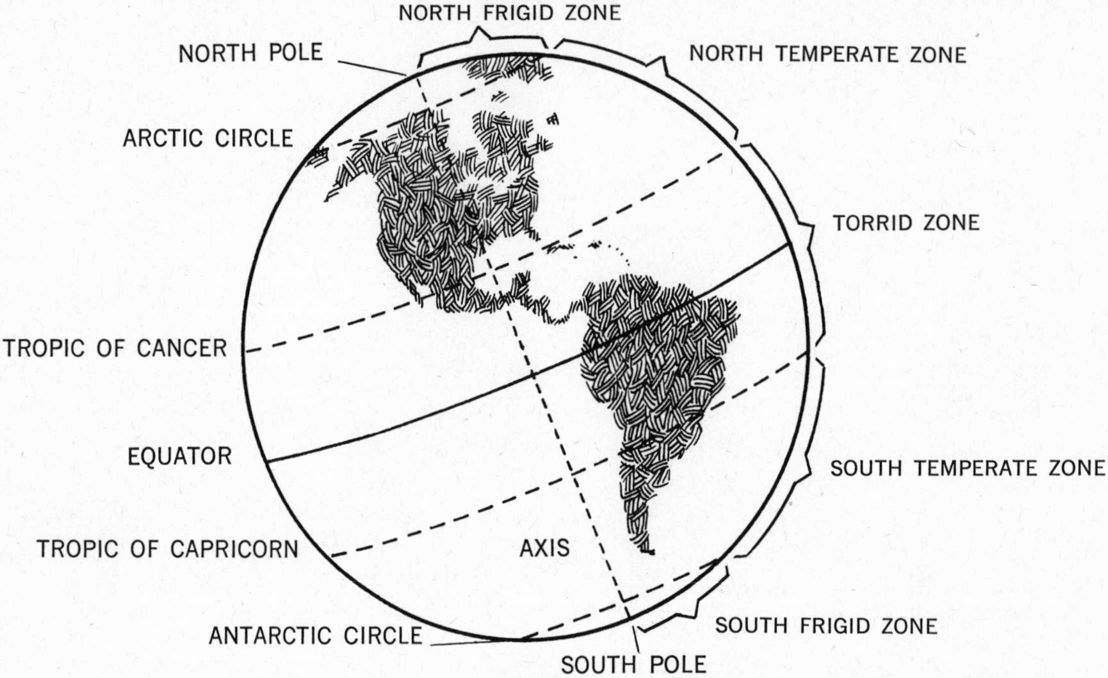

Now let us find out what happens to the temperature at one place during the hours from sunrise to sunset. At sunrise the sun is low in the east. At sunset it is low in the west. In both of these positions the sun's rays only graze the earth's surface producing a small rise in temperature. At noon, however, the sun is highest in the sky. Its rays are most direct, producing a larger increase in temperature. We can use the model surface again to show our position in relation to the sun for different hours of the day. At sunrise and sunset we are on line 1. At noon we are on line 3 and during the forenoon and afternoon we are on line 2.

You can test this yourself by taking temperature readings every two hours with the bulb-covered thermometer used in the previous experiment. Put it in a spot exposed to the sun all day, or you can take the readings in a shaded place outdoors. Do not go by a single day's readings because sometimes a special condition may alter the general pattern. For each time of day average the readings of a week or two at least. You will find that the "greenhouse" effect usually makes the highest temperatures come two or three hours after noon and not exactly at noon as you might expect. Also, to be a bit more scientific in this study, you should omit from your records all days that are not generally clear and fair. You will find that from hour to hour the position of the sun in the sky has an important effect upon temperature.

Perhaps you will wonder why we had to limit the conditions in these experiments? As we hinted before, there are other things or conditions that can affect the weather. One of these is the condition of the air, and the other is the water content of the air. The two are seldom completely separate in nature. So on we go to the story of air and water as weathermakers.

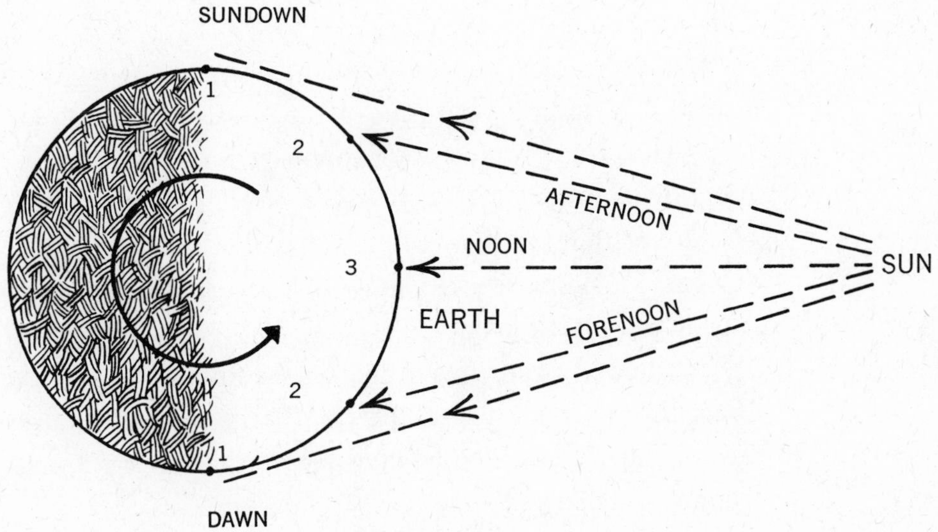

3. Air—the Earth's Invisible Cover

When you talk about the weather (and who does not?) you are talking about the air—its temperature, its movement and what it transports. Air is invisible. No one has ever seen it. That is fortunate because if we could see the air, we would see little else.

What is this substance we call air? Air is known to be a mixture of several gases, all of them odorless and colorless. That is the reason you cannot see air or detect it except by its feel. Let it blow against you and you will have no doubt that air is a real substance. If you would like to know a simple way to show that air is real, just catch some in a plastic bag.

If you press your finger against the bulging side of the bag, the air inside resists the push. This shows that even though air is made up of invisible gases, it is a real substance and takes up space.

Because air is real, it has weight. A cubic foot of air at sea level weighs a little more than one ounce, or about the same weight as nine pennies. How much does a roomful of air weigh? Suppose the room is 12 feet long, 12 feet wide and 10 feet high. You can find its air content in cubic feet by multiplying 12 x 12 x 10. The answer is 1440 cubic feet. If each cubic foot weights about one ounce and there are 16 ounces in a pound, you will find that this much air weighs about 90 pounds ($1440 \div 16 = 90$). So if a wind storm blows the equivalent of a roomful of air against you at 40 or 50 miles an hour, you'd better watch out. Better yet, stay indoors.

Have you ever gone out to play football and suddenly found yourself on the bottom of a pile of other players who had decided that you had run far enough with the ball? As each one got off your back, you could feel the pressure getting less and less. Think of the air at sea level as being on the bottom of a pile of air perhaps 1,000 miles high. Down at sea level the pressure of the air is tremendous, 15 pounds on every square inch of surface.

The higher up in the atmosphere you go, the lower the pressure becomes. The boy who was almost at the top of the football pile-up felt less pressure than you did at the bottom. People who climb high mountains or who fly in airplanes above 10,000 feet find breathing difficult, so they dress in special suits or wear pressurized masks. No doubt you have seen pictures of men who are training to become space explorers. In space there is no air, so special suits must be worn. The problems of space travellers are interesting, but right now we must keep our thinking within 10 miles of the earth's surface.

The lowest 15,000 feet (about 3 miles) of the earth's air ocean is the region where most weather changes take place.

You learned before how the sun can heat various parts

of the earth's surface unequally. Some of this heat is given up to the air above these surfaces. You probably have blown out the candles on a birthday cake. Perhaps you saw how the smoke continued to rise from the still-warm wicks of the candles. It was carried upward by the heated air. But why did the heated air rise? The reason is that it was *pushed* upward by the cooler air around it.

Cooled air moves downward. Have you ever noticed where the cooling unit is located in a refrigerator or even in an old-fashioned ice box? It is near the top. The cold air moving downward cools the food in the lower parts of the box. This is not the whole explanation. It tells us that cool air goes down and that it pushes up the warmer air. It does not explain why. To understand this fact, you should try a simple experiment. For the experiment you need an easily made piece of apparatus, as shown in the illustration. The picture shows you how to put it together with

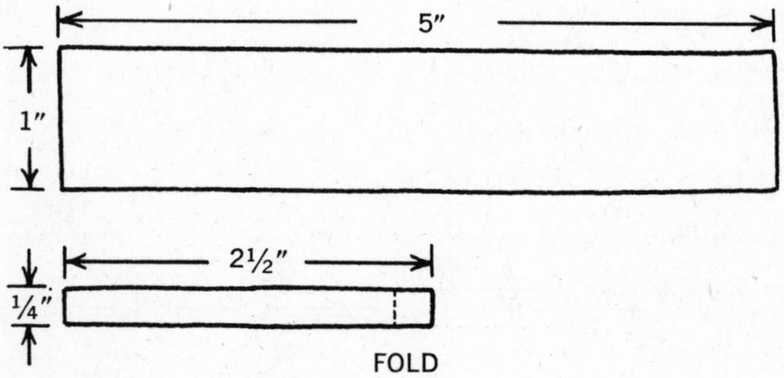

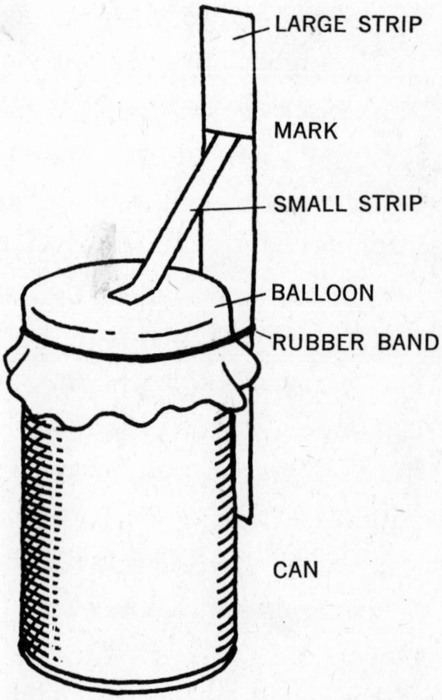

a fruit-juice can, a broken balloon, a rubber band, two small pieces of cardboard and a spot of rubber cement.

If you make this apparatus, here is how it will work. The can will be full of air. The balloon is free to move up or down, and whichever way it goes, the small piece of cardboard will move with it. The small piece of cardboard will act as a pointer on the scale on the larger piece of cardboard. What can we do to make the air in the can move the balloon? We will do this by heating and then by cooling the air.

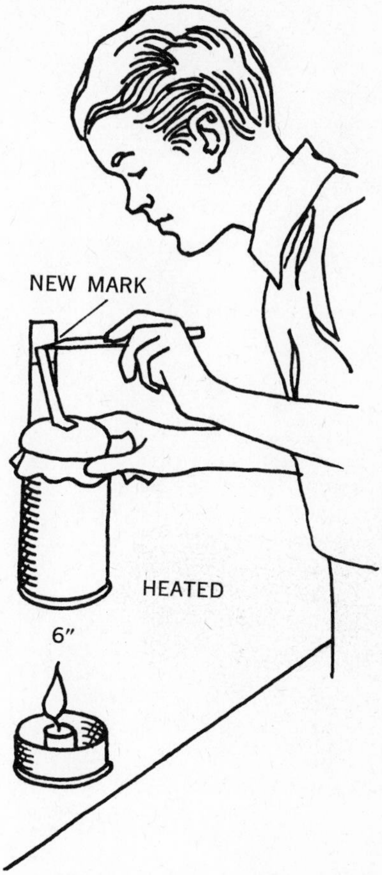

First, holding the top rim of the can, place the bottom of the can over a candle flame as the boy in the drawing is doing. Do you see how the top of the balloon begins to curve upward? In which direction does the pointer move? Second, allow the can to cool by placing it in a dish of crushed ice or by putting it into the ice-cube compartment of your refrigerator or into a deep-freeze unit. After a time, examine the device and notice the position of the balloon. Its surface seems to be curved downward and the pointer is lower on the scale.

This experiment shows you that heated air expands, and cooled air contracts. In both cases the amount of air in the can was the same because it was trapped. If the can had been open, some of the air would have escaped when the can was heated. There would have been less air inside the can than before, so what was left would have weighed less. If the can had been open and cooled, some extra air would have come into the can and the contents would have weighed more. Remember this while we take time out for a game of seesaw.

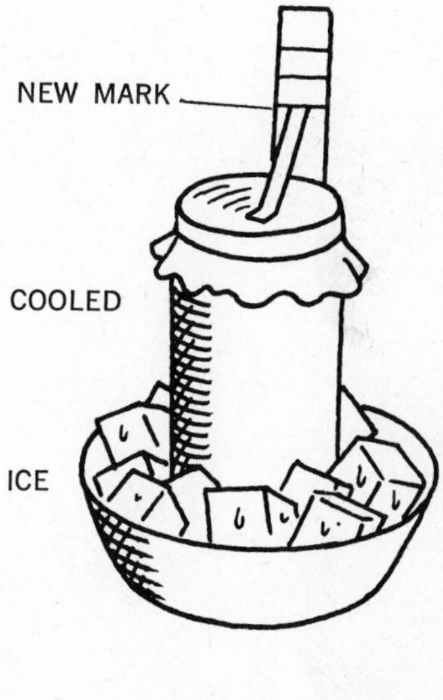

If you sit at one end of a seesaw and someone who is heavier sits at the opposite end, you will be the one who goes up. Let us imagine that there is a can of warm (light) air on one end of a seesaw and an equal-sized can of cool (heavy) air at the other end. Which can of air will be pushed upward? It is the one with the warmer air, of course, because that can is lighter. The same thing happens in nature. Since air in a region that is hot becomes lighter than normal, and air in a nearby region that is cool becomes heavier than normal, the warm air is pushed up by the cooler air.

As you can see, there is a circulation of the air, which may be on a small scale or on a large scale. The rising, warm air current is matched somewhere by a falling, colder air current. You may have had the experience of riding in an airplane that suddenly dropped 1,000 feet. Someone may have said later that it had gone into an air pocket. This is not correct. The plane did not drop, but it did move down rapidly in a cold air current. In open air there can be no pockets.

The cross currents, which flow more or less horizontally, are our winds and breezes. There are also winds high up in the sky. The speed and direction of the winds depend upon the size and location of differences in air temperature and pressure. Winds cannot be seen, but they can do things to show their presence and strength. You will read later how the strength of the wind and its direction can be measured.

The wind is like a conveyor belt. It carries smoke, dust, leaves, dirt, fumes, the seed of plants, germs, people's hats, and many other things. A hurricane wind is strong enough to lift off the roof of a house and carry it away. But of all the things the wind can carry, the most important is moisture.

Moisture in the air may be found as a gas called *water vapor*. It can be found as drops of rain or tiny droplets that make up clouds. It can be found as solid crystals of ice in certain types of clouds. In the next chapter you will find out more about water—the "secret ingredient" of weather.

4. Water—the Secret Ingredient

People sometimes complain about the uncomfortable weather in summer, only to be told, "It isn't the heat. It's the humidity." *Humidity* refers to the secret ingredient of the air, its moisture content. Although the percentages of the main gases in the air—nitrogen (78 percent) and oxygen (21 percent)—do not change much, the moisture in it may change from hour to hour. Where does the moisture come from? Where does it go? What does it do?

The moisture in the air is just one part of a great "Water Cycle"—that is, a kind of continuous process in which many things, including you, have an important part. Water exists everywhere in one form or another and, without it, life could not go on. The main supply of water is in the five oceans (Atlantic, Pacific, Indian, Arctic, Antarctic) and many smaller bodies of water. Much of the earth's water is caught in the great polar ice caps and glaciers.

Much of it is in inland waterways such as lakes, rivers and canals. Tremendous amounts of water are hidden in the soil, in plants, in animals and in the atmosphere. What will bring it out of its hiding places?

You know water best as a liquid. In this form you drink it, wash with it and swim in it. Yet water is not always a liquid. Sometimes it changes into an invisible gas, water vapor. You have seen this happen whenever you have boiled water. If you do not remember seeing bubbles appear at the bottom of the pot, look for them the next time you boil water. Then try something else. Keep watching the water as it boils. It isn't just bubbling. It is disappearing. Keep on watching, and you will see the water level drop lower and lower. Where did it go? Think about it.

Boiling is not the only way to make water disappear. It can happen when water is left in an open dish. If you want to prove that the water disappears just fill a saucer with water and let it stand in a place where it will not be disturbed. From time to time, check the level of the water. In a few days, the water will have vanished. Think also about the way that clothes are washed and hung up to dry. At first they are full of water, but in a short time they are dry. This is called *evaporation* (eh-vap-uh-*ray*-shun).

Evaporation is the slow way in which water changes into water vapor. Boiling is a faster process. Both require heat, but, in the case of boiling, the heat is applied in a large amount for a short time. The boiling point of water at sea level is 212° F. Higher up where the air pressure is less, boiling takes place at lower temperatures. You can tell that evaporation also requires heat because you shiver when you climb out of a swimming pool on a breezy day. The breeze helps evaporate the water on your body. Since the heat needed to make it evaporate comes from your body, you become cold enough to shiver. The faster the air blows over a wet surface, the faster evaporation takes place. Also, the higher the temperature, and the larger the surface exposed to the air, the more rapid the evaporation. Thus water disappears into the air.

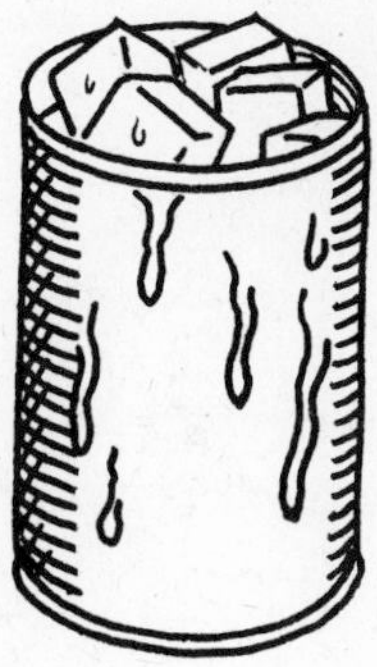

A good magician doesn't only make things disappear—he brings them back again. The magic of the weather is that the water vapor unseen in the air can reappear not only as water but sometimes as snowflakes, sometimes as bits of ice. These changes take place often but they go on high in the sky. To make them happen close at hand just fill a glass or a shiny metal can with crushed ice. Soon you will see drops of water forming on the outside of the container. Where did this water come from?

On the pipes of the freezing unit of your refrigerator, you can find another example. Where did the water that formed the ice on that unit come from? If you say, "From the air," you are correct. The process is called *condensation* (kon-den-*say*-shun). Do you know how it happens ?

Think of the air as a sponge. You probably have used a sponge and know that after it has soaked up a certain amount of water, it will hold no more. So it is with the air. At a particular temperature, air can hold only a certain amount of water, as shown:

Temperature	Total amount of water a roomful * of air can hold
40° F.	about 5 ounces or ⅓ pound
50° F.	about 8 ounces (½ pound)
60° F.	about 12 ounces (¾ pound)
70° F.	about 16 ounces (1 pound)
80° F.	about 22 ounces or 1⅓ pounds
90° F.	about 29 ounces or 1¾ pounds

* A room 10 feet long, 10 feet wide and 10 feet high.

If you lower the temperature of the air enough, it will have to give up some of the water it is holding. Air is less and less of a sponge as its temperature decreases. So, if you want to condense water out of the air, cool it. In nature this happens in several ways. When it happens clouds form.

Clouds may form when warm, moist air rises from the ground (or near the ground) to a higher level where it becomes cooled. Clouds may also form when a mass of warm, moist air mixes with a mass of cooler air. You have probably made clouds like this simply by exhaling your breath on a cold day. Remember that whenever a cloud forms, the droplets condense on something. If you have ever looked at a beam of sunlight you know that the air has a tremendous number of tiny dust particles floating around in it. They may be too small to be seen except in a strong beam of light, but they are there, always ready to be used by water vapor that needs particles on which to condense.

CONDENSATION CHART

Description of the event	How vapor is cooled	Air temperature at which vapor condenses	Place where vapor condenses	Form in which vapor condenses
Cloud forms when you breathe out into cold air	By mixing with cold air	Above 32° F.	In the air in front of your mouth	Drops of water
Cloud forms near spout of kettle in which water is boiling	By mixing with colder air	Above 32° F.	In the air about an inch away from the spout	Drops of water
Eyeglasses cloud over when you enter a warm house from the cold outdoors	By contact with cold glass	Above 32° F.	On the glass	Drops of water
The outside of pitcher of ice water "sweats"	By contact with cold pitcher	Above 32° F.	On the pitcher	Drops of water
Inside of window pane clouds over when it is cold outdoors	By contact with cold window	Above 32° F.	On the inside of the glass	Drops of water
Grass is covered with dew on a cold night	By contact with the cold grass	Above 32° F.	On the grass	Drops of water
Fog forms over a city	By loss of heat to the city	Above 32° F.	In the air right above the streets	Drops of water
Cumulus clouds develop over a hot region	By loss of heat due to expansion of rising air	Above 32° F.	High in the atmosphere	Drops of water
Frost forms on the inside of your window	By contact with *very* cold window	Below 32° F.	On the glass	Crystals of ice
Frost forms on containers in freezer bins in super markets	By contact with *very* cold containers	Below 32° F.	On the containers	Crystals of ice
Frost forms on the ground	By contact with *very* cold ground	Below 32° F.	On the ground	Crystals of ice
Cirrus clouds appear in the sky	By *great* loss of heat due to expansion of rising air	Below 32° F.	Very high in the atmosphere	Crystals of ice

The Condensation Chart lists twelve common ways in which condensation may take place.

Evaporation and condensation are two of the three parts of the Water Cycle. A cycle, as you know, is something that happens again and again. The third part of the Water Cycle is *precipitation*. Precipitation means falling down, and the precipitation of water refers to falling rain, snow, hail, and sleet. Where and how these types of precipitation form is shown in the Precipitation Chart.

Just to be sure we understand it, let us go through the

PRECIPITATION CHART
The Different Forms in Which Water Falls from Clouds

What is its name?	What does it look like?	What is it?	How does it form?	At what temperature does it form?	From which clouds does it fall?
RAIN	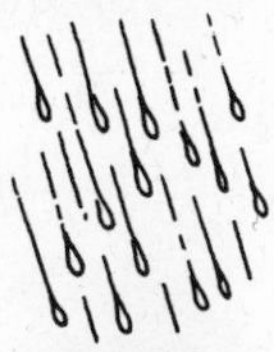	Water in liquid form	Tiny cloud droplets fuse to form larger drops. To fall, raindrop must be at least 1/125 of an inch across.	Above 32° F.	Altocumulus (drizzle) Altostratus (light rain) Stratocumulus (drizzle) Stratus (drizzle) Nimbostratus (steady rain) Cumulonimbus (heavy rain for short time)
SNOW		Water in solid form	Water vapor condenses into solid form without first becoming a liquid.	Far below 32° F. Usually between 10° F. above zero to 10° F. below zero.	Altocumulus (snow flurry) Altostratus (light snow) Stratocumulus (snow flurry) Stratus (snow flurry) Nimbostratus (steady snow) Cumulonimbus (heavy snow for short time)
SLEET		Water in solid form	In falling through a layer of freezing air, rain drops become ice drops.	At or slightly below 32° F.	Stratus Nimbostratus Cumulonimbus
HAIL		Layers of frozen water	Raindrop freezes. Second layer of water collects on ice. Second layer freezes. Third layer collects. Buildup continues until hailstone falls.	At or slightly below 32° F.	Cumulonimbus Hail usually comes with thunderstorms and sometimes with tornadoes.
DEW		Water in liquid form	Air containing water vapor cools by contact with cold objects on ground. Water vapor condenses right on the objects.	Above 32° F.	Dew does not fall from clouds. It does not fall from anywhere. It condenses from air that touches cold objects.
FROST		Water in solid form	Same as above but water vapor condenses right into solid form.	Below 32° F.	Same explanation as for dew.

whole water cycle once more. Of course we could start anywhere, but let us begin with evaporation. This is the process that puts millions of tons of moisture into the atmosphere. During the process of evaporation, water vapor comes from oceans, lakes, rivers, our skin, drying wash and any other open, wet area. Living plants and animals also add water vapor to the atmosphere. This invisible vapor lifts heat energy into the air. Moving air currents and winds carry this energy-filled vapor all around the world.

Wherever and whenever moisture-laden air is circulated to a place where it cools off enough, condensation takes place. During condensation the invisible water vapor changes back into visible liquid or solid form. At this time the heat energy picked up by the vapor is released to the new surroundings. This energy adds to the violence of storms. Precipitation does not always follow condensation, but when it does, water in solid or liquid form drops back to the earth. For example, when one inch of rain falls on an area the size of Chicago (200 square miles) about 15 million tons of water come down!

As we pointed out before, the atmosphere is like an endless chain of buckets or a conveyor belt. Where evaporation takes place the "buckets" pick up water vapor and energy. Circulation brings these "buckets" to another part of the earth. Then condensation and precipitation dump the "buckets" and the water and energy are returned to the earth. Remember that no matter how many times the Water Cycle goes around—and it never stops—the total amount of water on the earth and in its atmosphere remains about the same. However, much of it may be held captive for a long time in icepacks and glaciers. If all of these were to melt, the level of the oceans would be raised several hundred feet. In that case much of the most valuable areas of our country and of the world would be flooded and lost for many centuries.

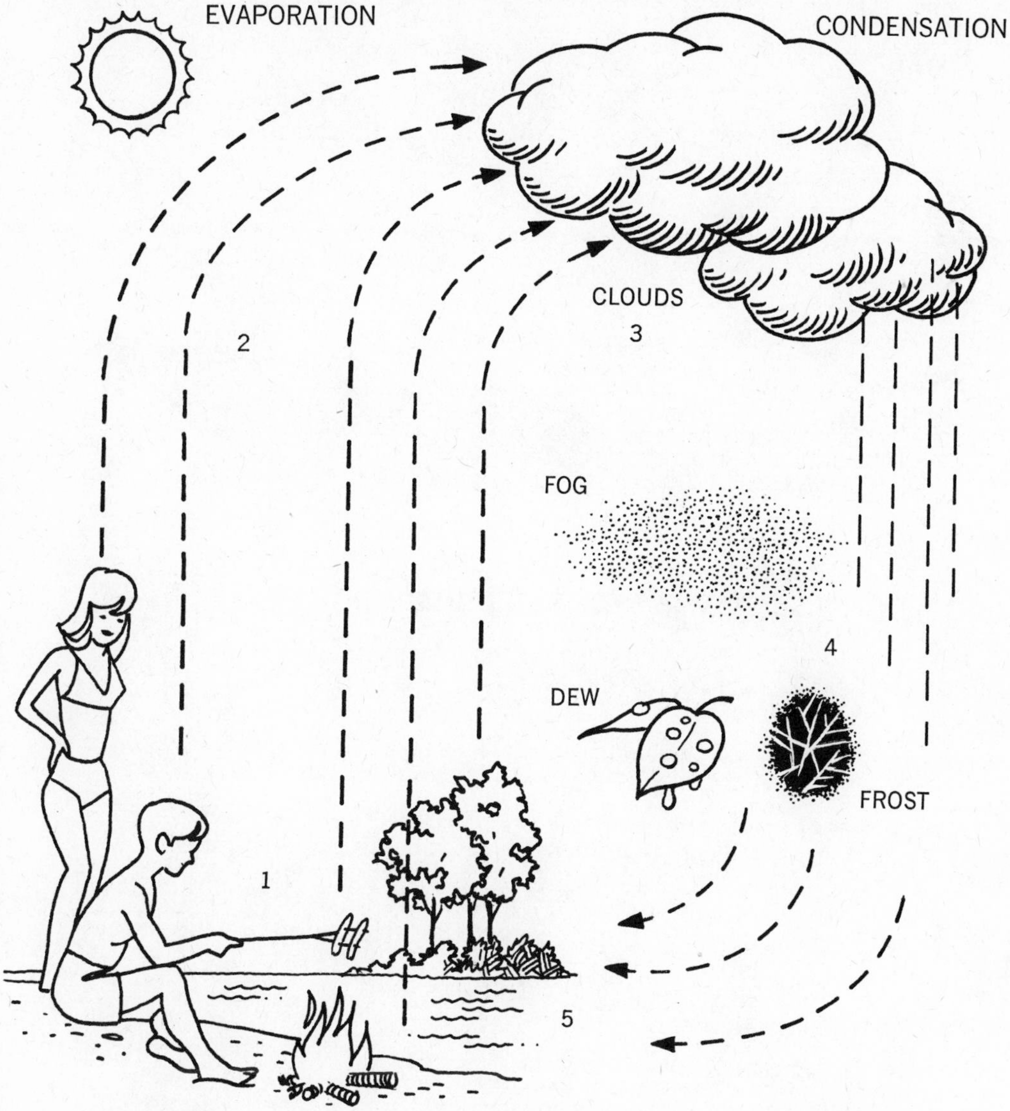

THE WATER CYCLE

WAYS IN WHICH WATER ENTERS AND LEAVES THE ATMOSPHERE

1 WATER EVAPORATES FROM OCEANS, LAKES, RIVERS, BROOKS, PUDDLES, MOIST EARTH, FROM LIVING THINGS AND BURNING FUEL

2 VAPOR IS CARRIED UP BY ASCENDING CURRENTS

3 VAPOR CONDENSES IN THESE FORMS

4 CONDENSED WATER IN CLOUDS MAY FALL TO EARTH AS RAIN, SNOW, HAIL OR SLEET

5 WATER RETURNS TO PLANTS, ANIMALS, PEOPLE, SOIL, OCEANS, ETC.

5. Clouds—the Weather Messengers

In the past, people used to depend upon the clouds for signs of coming weather. Today, you can get weather news easily by reading a newspaper, listening to the radio, watching television and, in many cities, by dialing a special telephone number. In spite of this great progress in reporting, cloud watching is still an extremely important method of getting weather news, and weathermen make it a regular part of their work.

Each type of cloud carries a message, giving advance notice of coming changes in the weather. From such cloud clues you can get a fairly good idea of what kind of weather to expect in the next 24 to 48 hours. However, if you want to be able to read these messages, you have to study the clouds themselves.

The simplest message is the one that comes from a perfectly clear sky. As long as the sky remains clear, you can be sure that very little condensation is going on up above. This means, of course, that there is no chance of rain or snow.

The first cloud you see marks the beginning of a change. Where a cloud appears suddenly from out of nowhere, condensation is beginning at that very place. If the cloud mushrooms upward, it indicates the presence of a rising current of air. A cloud that spreads out sideways shows that there is little up or down air movement in that place. If more condensation than evaporation occurs, the cloud grows bigger. If the reverse is true, the cloud becomes smaller and may actually vanish. All the fascinating figures and forms that you see in the clouds are the result of these never-ending changes.

As more and more water accumulates in a cloud, it gets bigger, drops lower in the sky and becomes thicker. Less sunlight comes through the cloud, and it darkens. By contrast, the thinner edges are much brighter because they allow more sunlight to come through. Even the darkest and most menacing clouds are rimmed with a silvery border. From this comes the saying, "Every cloud has a silver lining." You may have heard people use this expression to try to brighten the spirit of someone in a dark mood.

Sometimes you may see clouds drifting across the sky like ships at sea. You can tell that they are moving by comparing them with hill tops, buildings, towers, telephone poles, trees or other high objects on the ground. The change in size of such clouds may be due to their own growth or shrinkage, or it may be an illusion created as they come closer to you or move farther away.

The direction and speed of a cloud is a clue to the direction and speed of the air current that is carrying the cloud. The patterns of the cloud formations are clues to the manner in which the air currents are circulating in the region. Just as winds may set up ripples on the surface of a lake, so too may air currents give a rippled appearance to cloud formations. Helter-skelter air movements are revealed by swirling clouds.

Several things will help you determine the height of clouds. The highest clouds are thin and are almost always white except at sunrise and sunset. At such times, they are the first to pick up sunrise colors and the last to lose the glowing hues of sunset. Fog, the cloud form nearest the earth, is the one you can walk in. You don't need clues to detect its presence. You can spot a fog at a distance by the way it hugs the ground. In general, low clouds are flat, wide-spread and dark gray in color. When clouds at different heights move across the sky, the low clouds block out the view of the higher ones.

All in all, the clouds tell many things. They tell you in what regions and at what heights condensation is going on. They show the direction and speed of unseen air currents. They disclose whether these currents are flowing gently or moving violently. The shades of clouds, ranging from white to near black, reveal whether they are storing much or little water.

Weathermen around the world, to make sure that they understand one another, have adopted an international system of cloud identification. Clouds are grouped in two ways—on the basis of appearance and on the basis of height. Of the common clouds, the highest are delicate, feathery-looking curly wisps. They are named *cirrus* (*sih*-rus) *clouds,* from the Latin word meaning curl. Although they may be moving at speeds as high as 200 miles per hour, they often seem to be going more slowly or even standing still. This is because of their great altitude. Cirrus clouds are usually four or more miles above the earth. This makes them visible to ground observers up to one hundred miles away.

CIRRUS Ci

At four or five miles above the earth, temperatures are far below freezing, and the clouds are made up mainly

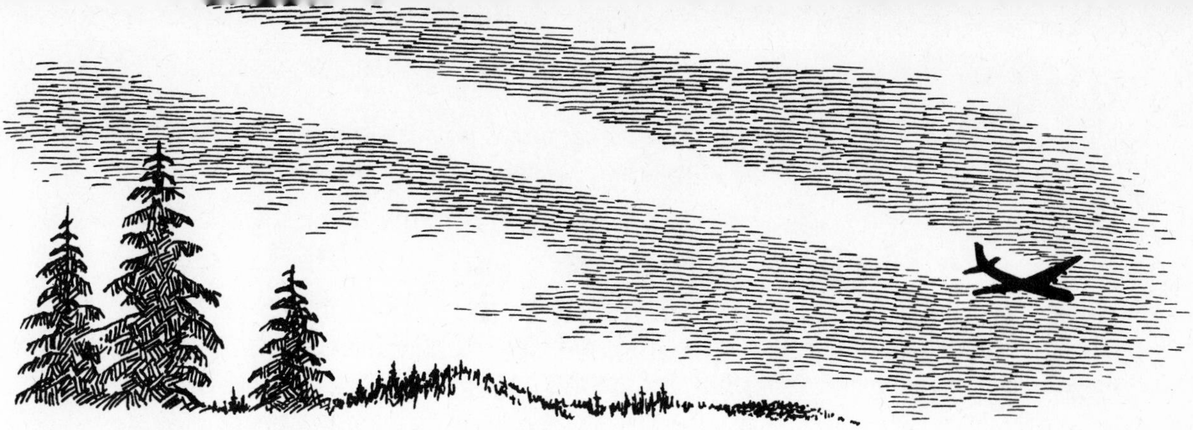

of tiny ice crystals spread out very thinly. You might find only one small crystal in a thimbleful of cirrus cloud. Because the crystals are so light, they are tossed about by the slightest shift of air, up or down, or from side to side. Sometimes the flowing streams of crystals give the cirrus clouds the appearance of wind-blown tails of horses. Thus, they are nicknamed "mares' tails." No precipitation is likely to fall from cirrus clouds. The crystals in them are too light to drop. When you see them, you can be quite certain that the weather will remain fair, unless they begin to thicken.

A jet plane, streaking through the sky, leaves a trail of man-made cirrus clouds. The water vapor in the exhaust gases condenses into ice crystals. These trails are shown in the picture above.

Another type of cloud is one of even thickness and gray color resembling a blanket. Because of the form of this cloud, it is named *stratus* (*stray*-tus) from the Latin word for "something spreading out." It may be found spread out in a layer, anywhere from the ground up to a height of about one mile. If it is on the ground, it is called fog. The fact that it is arranged in a layer indicates that there is very little up or down movement of air. Through stratus clouds, the sun and the moon show up only as dim spots of light.

Since stratus clouds are in relatively warm regions of the atmosphere, they are composed mainly of tiny drops of

STRATUS St

water. A teaspoonful of this cloud material contains about 5 billion microscopic drops of water. It would take you more than 30 years, counting 5 each second, to tally that number of drops. Because they are so very fine, they do not fall to earth easily. Depending upon the time of year, if precipitation does occur, it generally is in the form of light drizzle or snow flurries. As you watch, if the stratus layer drops lower and darkens, the chance for rain or snow increases. When this happens, the sun or moon spot grows fainter. However, if the reverse occurs, and the light spot becomes brighter, the weather trend is to fair.

A third kind of cloud formation is the *cumulus* (*kyoom*-yoo-lus) *cloud*. In Latin, cumulus means "heap" or "pile." Cumulus clouds are very conspicuous because they look like puffs of pure white cotton. They are born when updrafts of air reach into cooler regions where water vapor begins to condense. The flat bottom of the cloud marks the altitude at which this process begins. As condensation continues into the higher levels, the cloud material piles up. Since the cloud grows in this rising current, its structure is mainly vertical.

CUMULUS Cu

In the middle of hot days, it is not unusual to find these little puffs hovering over heated regions of land. At such times, when a sailor on the sea sights a lone cumulus cloud in a clear sky, he knows that there probably is an island right under the cloud. Most cumulus clouds appear in the sky at heights ranging from one quarter of a mile to about four miles. At the lower levels, they are composed mainly of drops of water. If the updraft reaches high enough, some of the vapor may condense as ice crystals. Except for a rare sprinkling, no precipitation is likely to fall from cumulus clouds. These are "fair weather" clouds.

On hot summer afternoons, when air currents often zoom upward for miles and miles, cumulus clouds may mushroom into another variety known as *cumulonimbus* (kyoom-yoo-low-*nim*-bus) *clouds*. From such clouds come the violent thunder and lightning storms that may spoil your plans for a summer afternoon outing. The name cumulonimbus is a combination of the word cumulus (pile) and the Latin word nimbus, meaning "rainstorm cloud." More commonly, cumulonimbus clouds are known as "thunderheads." They are the giants of the cloud family. Starting with flat bases as close to the earth as a quarter of a mile, some of these giants may tower upward as high as four miles or more. At the top, where the rising air column begins to flatten out, the cloud takes the shape of the pointed end of a blacksmith's anvil. As a matter of fact, the point indicates the direction in which the thunderhead is moving.

CUMULONIMBUS Cb

Within each cumulonimbus cloud a terrific churning goes on, as hot air, cold air, raindrops and ice crystals are tossed about. In the midst of all this commotion, the friction generates electricity. The cloud may become charged with as much as fifty million volts of electricity. To obtain a similar voltage with flashlight cells, you would have to place about thirty-five million of them end to end.

When you see a thunderhead developing in the distance, you can be fairly sure that these things will happen. The sky will darken. The winds will become more violent. Lightning will flash, and thunder will rumble. By counting the number of seconds between the time you see the flash and hear the resulting thunder, you can tell roughly how far away the storm center is. Every five seconds of your count represents a distance of one mile. In other words, if you count fifteen seconds, the thunderhead is about three miles away from you.

Once the storm actually rages around you, bucketsful of rain and sometimes hail will fall. When you see a thunderstorm approaching, it is wise to take certain precautions to avoid being struck by lightning. Try to find shelter in a house or an automobile. If you cannot get to a shelter in time, stretch out flat on the ground away from trees. If you are swimming or boating, get back to shore immediately.

Just as cumulus clouds can grow into cumulonimbus storm clouds, so also cirrus clouds can develop into other forms. Cirrus clouds may change into *cirrostratus* (sih-roh-*strayt*-us) *clouds*. As you can tell from the name, the cirrostratus is a form of cirrus cloud that spreads out in layers at a height of about four miles. As more and more ice crystals fill the spaces between the isolated wisps of cirrus, the transformation into cirrostratus takes place. As it develops, the cirrostratus looks more and more like a milky cobweb spread across the sky. Although the sun and moon can be seen clearly through this veil, they are both surrounded by rings of light. These *halos* are formed when light passes through the ice crystals of the cloud.

CIRROSTRATUS Cs

Cirrus clouds may also become *cirrocumulus* (sih-roh-*kyoom*-yoo-lus) *clouds*. In almost all respects, cirrocumulus clouds are similar to the other cirrus types. They are made up of ice crystals and form about four miles above the ground. The difference is that they are clusters of little white puffs that are arranged in such a way as to resemble markings on a mackerel fish. For this reason, the sky in which they appear is called a "mackerel sky."

CIRROCUMULUS Cc

No precipitation falls from any of this family of high cirrus clouds. If they thicken and drop into warmer regions of the atmosphere, they may change gradually into grayer-looking stratus clouds. Such a change is a certain sign of the approach of rain or snow, depending upon the season.

In the middle portion of the atmosphere, from about one to four miles high, you can see members of the *"alto"* family of clouds, named after the Latin word for high. *Altostratus* (al-toh-*stray*-tus) *clouds* are gray-blue in color and are composed of a mixture of ice crystals and water

ALTOSTRATUS As

drops. The sun or moon may be seen through these clouds as a dim patch of light. A storm is likely to be approaching if these clouds darken toward the west. There is also a possibility of steady rain or snow falling from the altostratus clouds themselves.

Another "alto" cloud is the *altocumulus* (al-toh-*kyoom*-yoo-lus) *cloud*. It resembles the cirrocumulus but consists of drops of water rather than crystals of ice. The individual puffs also are larger. On occasion, they cluster together to form a "herring-bone" pattern. Through these clouds, the sun or moon seem to be rimmed by a band of yellowish or bluish color known as a *corona*. A decrease in the size of the corona is an indication that wet weather is coming soon.

ALTOCUMULUS Ac

Sometimes low-level clouds appear in the sky, lined up like ripples in corrugated cardboard. Because they combine the flatness of the stratus cloud with the puffiness of the cumulus, they are known by the combined name *stratocumulus* (stray-toh-*kyoom*-yoo-lus) *clouds*. They are made up mainly of drops of water. Although a drizzle or snowflurry may fall from them, they are not really rain clouds. When you see stratocumulus clouds, watch them carefully because you can expect the weather to change. They can either break up, bringing clearing skies, or join together to form into rain clouds.

STRATOCUMULUS Sc

True rain clouds are the easiest to recognize. They are heavy, low-hanging, dark-gray stratus clouds. You can probably name these clouds from this description. They are *nimbostratus* (nim-boh-*stray*-tus) *clouds,* made up of ice crystals and drops of water. They generally cover the entire sky at an average height of half a mile. Within a few hours after you see nimbostratus clouds, you can expect several days of steady rain or snow or both. The long period of bad weather brought by this type of cloud is in sharp contrast to the "easy come, easy go" character of

NIMBOSTRATUS Ns

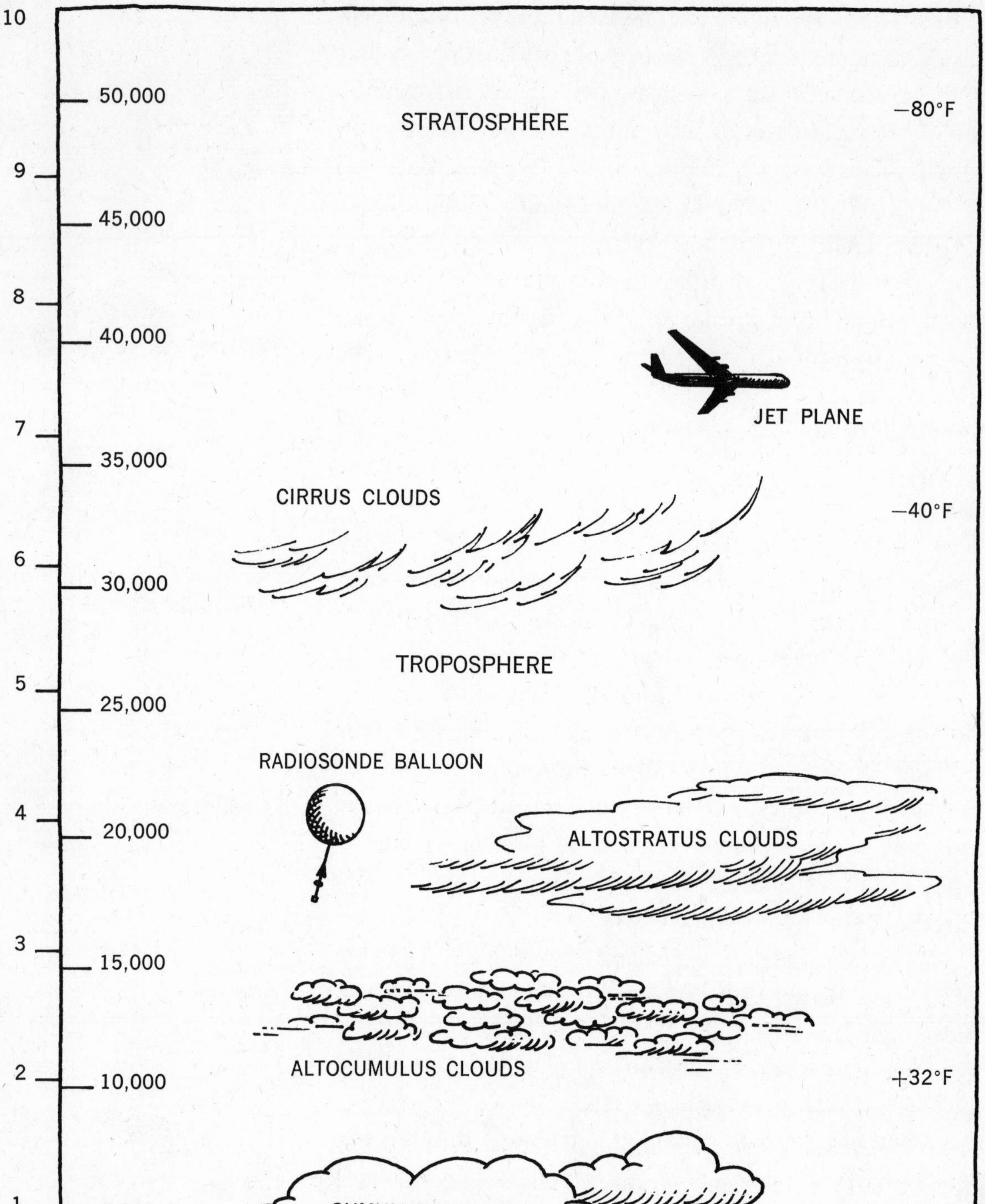
10
50,000
STRATOSPHERE
−80°F
9
45,000
8
40,000
JET PLANE
7
35,000
CIRRUS CLOUDS
−40°F
6
30,000
TROPOSPHERE
5
25,000
RADIOSONDE BALLOON
4
20,000
ALTOSTRATUS CLOUDS
3
15,000
ALTOCUMULUS CLOUDS
2
10,000
+32°F
1
5,000
CUMULUS CLOUDS
MILES
FEET
SEA LEVEL
+70°F

the flashy cumulonimbus. As more and more water gathers in stratus, altostratus, or stratocumulus clouds, any of these can grow into nimbostratus.

CLOUD CHART

Cloud name	Abbrev.	What are the clouds made of?	What may fall from the clouds?	What weather do the clouds forecast?	How high are the clouds?	What is the symbol?
CIRRUS	Ci	Ice crystals	Nothing	**Fair,** but Rain or Snow if clouds thicken.	4 miles or more	
CIRROSTRATUS	Cs	Ice crystals	Nothing	**Fair** if they break up into cirrocumulus.	4 miles or more	
CIRROCUMULUS	Cc	Ice crystals	Nothing	**Rain** if clouds thicken and lower.	4 miles or more	
ALTOCUMULUS	Ac	Drops of water	Drizzle or snow flurry	**Rain** if corona around sun or moon decreases.	1 to 4 miles	
ALTOSTRATUS	As	Ice and water	Light rain or snow	**Storm** if clouds darken toward the west.	1 to 4 miles	
STRATOCUMULUS	Sc	Drops of water	Drizzle or snow flurries	**Changing weather.**	¼ to 1 mile	
STRATUS	St	Drops of water	Drizzle or snow flurries	**Fair** weather, if clouds get smaller.	0 to 1 mile	
NIMBOSTRATUS	Ns	Ice and water	Steady rain or snow	**Long** rainy stretch.	0 to 1 mile	
CUMULUS	Cu	Drops of water	Nothing	Generally **fair.**	¼ to 4 miles	
CUMULONIMBUS	Cb	Ice and water	Heavy rain, snow or hail	**Thunderstorms.**	¼ to 4 miles	

Now you have been introduced by name and description to ten major types of clouds. Within each type many variations occur. For instance, a "Cloud Code Chart" prepared by the United States Weather Bureau shows pictures of thirty-six different types of low-, middle-, and high-level clouds. You can obtain this chart by writing to the Superintendent of Documents, United States Government Printing Office, Washington, D.C. 20402.

To watch the exciting story of the clouds, you do not pay any kind of admission fee. All you have to do is go out and watch the sky. Once you've learned the code and mastered the clues, you will be amazed at the wide variety of messages that the clouds will bring you.

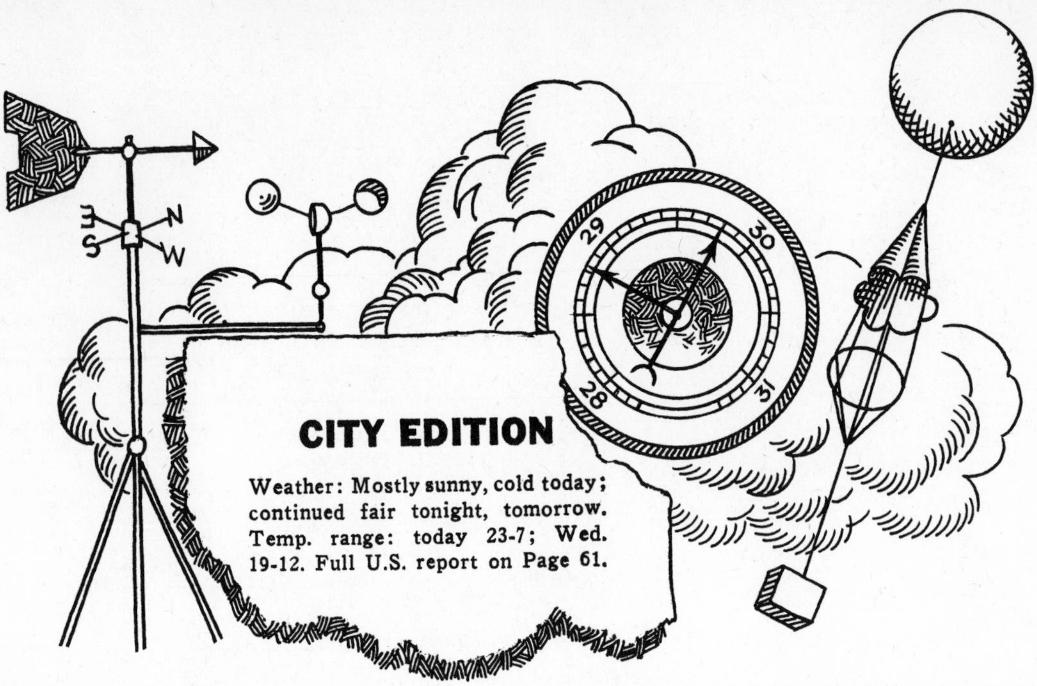
N
S
W
E
29
30
28
31
CITY EDITION
Weather: Mostly sunny, cold today; continued fair tonight, tomorrow. Temp. range: today 23-7; Wed. 19-12. Full U.S. report on Page 61.

6. Keeping Track of the Weather

Every change in weather, no matter how slight or how great, is the result of one or more changes in the condition of the atmosphere. By recording these changes as they take place across the country and by following them carefully, the weatherman finds out how the weather pattern is developing. He then makes a forecast of what the weather is likely to be within the next few hours or within the next few days.

You can observe many of these changes without the use of special instruments. When the temperature of the air goes up or drops rapidly, you can sense the difference. Also, increasing humidity makes you feel uncomfortable. From the movement of smoke out of chimneys, and the fluttering of flags, you can estimate which way and how fast the wind is blowing. As described in the previous chapter, the shifting patterns of clouds in the sky reveal regions of condensation and the flow of air currents. When it rains, it isn't hard to tell whether it is raining "cats and dogs" or just sprinkling. Similarly, you can see when a gentle snowfall is developing into a blizzard or the other way around.

How far can we trust our senses as weather instruments? In judging types of clouds, we are limited to those we can see. However, in judging other conditions, we run into two main problems. First, we cannot notice slight changes in such things as temperature and humidity. Only marked or rapid changes impress us. Second, a drop in temperature that may make one person uncomfortably cold may not bother someone else. It is for reasons such as these that the weatherman prefers to use instruments to keep track of changes. Some instruments have another advantage. As automatic, self-recording devices, they can stand watch twenty-four hours a day.

Measuring Temperature

No doubt you have used a *thermometer* to measure temperature. The word "thermometer" comes from the Greek words *therme* meaning "heat," and *metron* meaning "measure." To make a thermometer suitable for ordinary weather work the manufacturer uses a sealed glass tube with a little bulb blown out at one end. The bulb is filled with some liquid material. If the liquid is silvery it is probably mercury. If the liquid is red or blue, it may be colored alcohol. These liquids expand faster than the glass of the tube. When the bulb warms up, the liquid moves out of the bulb and into the tube. The warmer the bulb gets, the longer the column of liquid grows. When the bulb cools off, the liquid contracts back into it, and the column grows shorter.

To mark the scale on the thermometer, the bulb first is

placed in contact with melting ice. The point to which the liquid contracts is numbered thirty-two degrees. Then the bulb is placed in the steam of boiling water. The point to which the liquid expands is numbered two hundred and twelve degrees. The space between these two points is divided into equal parts. These markings are extended also below the freezing point and above the boiling point to complete the scale. Every tenth degree is numbered. If the space between the numbers is divided into five parts, then each line stands for two degrees. If it is divided into ten parts, then each line stands for one degree. In other words, when you see the liquid in the ordinary thermometer at the point shown in the diagram, the temperature reading is sixty-eight degrees. This is considered to be the room temperature that is comfortable for most people.

The *Fahrenheit* (*Far*-un-hyte) scale, just described, was invented in 1714 by Gabriel Fahrenheit, a German physicist. In setting up his scale, Fahrenheit thought that the lowest temperature was that of a mixture of ice and salt. He called this zero degrees. The freezing point of plain water turned out to be thirty-two degrees higher. As an upper point, Fahrenheit used what he thought was the unchanging temperature of the human body, which he designated as one hundred degrees. (We know now that the average normal body temperature is about ninety-eight and six-tenths degrees.) On this basis, the boiling point of water turns out to be two hundred and twelve degrees.

About twenty-eight years after Fahrenheit established his scale, Anders Celsius (*Sel*-sih-us), a Swedish astronomer, invented another type of scale. On the Celsius scale (also called the *centigrade* [*sent*-ih-grayd] scale) the freezing point of plain water is marked zero degrees and its boiling point is one hundred degrees.

You can change from one system to another with a simple calculation. To go from Fahrenheit to centigrade, sub-

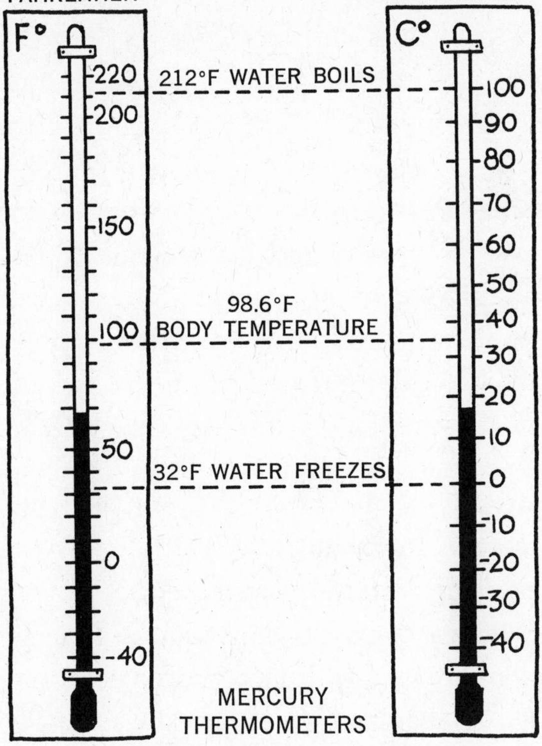

MERCURY THERMOMETERS

$$C° = \frac{F° - 32}{1.8}$$

$$F° = 1.8 \times C° + 32$$

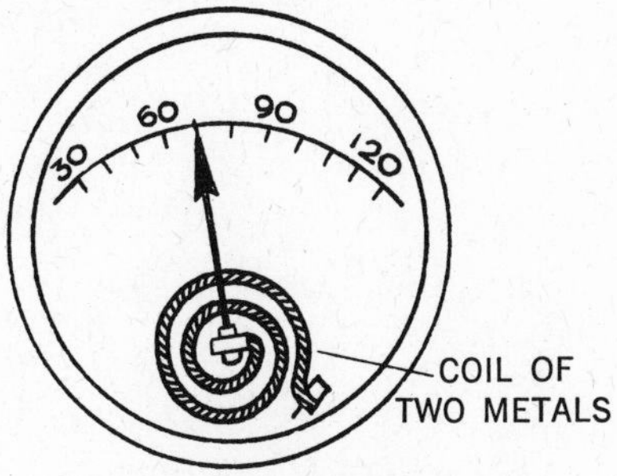

DIAL THERMOMETER

tract thirty-two from the Fahrenheit reading and divide the remainder by 1.8. To change the other way, multiply the centigrade reading by 1.8 and then add 32. In giving a temperature it is important to indicate by an F. or a C. after the degrees whether the scale is Fahrenheit or centigrade.

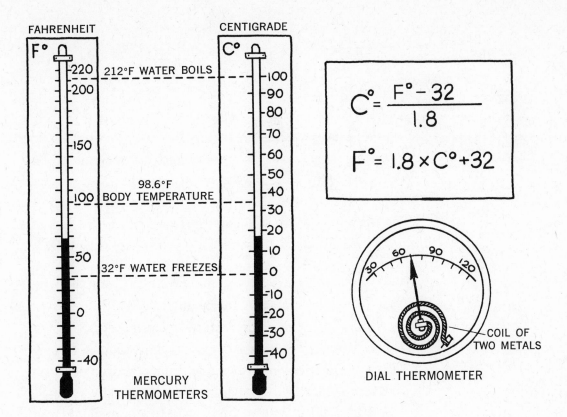

Another kind of thermometer, known as the *dial thermometer,* is shown in the illustration. The heart of this instrument is a coiled spiral strip of two different metals welded together. Because one metal expands and contracts more than the other when heated or cooled, the coil winds up and unwinds as the temperature varies. This action moves the pointer clockwise or counterclockwise. The advantage of the dial thermometer is that it does not break easily. However, it is not as accurate as a good mer-

THERMOGRAPH

cury thermometer. Both thermometers give only the temperature at the moment the reading is taken.

A more complete temperature recording device is the *thermograph* (*ther*-moh-graf). In this instrument a piece of paper mounted on a revolving drum is moved continuously by a clock. The temperature is measured by a curved metal tube filled with alcohol. The tube straightens out when the alcohol gets warm and expands. It curls up again when the alcohol cools and contracts. Attached to the moving end of the curved tube is a pen, which marks the changes on the paper as the drum turns. Some thermographs can make a continuous temperature record for every minute of an entire week.

It is interesting to know that thermometers, no matter how they work, have a common origin. They are all based on the one first devised in 1593 by the famous Italian scientist Galileo (gal-ih-*lay*-oh).

Measuring Relative Humidity

Temperature records alone are not enough for good weather forecasting. We must also know something about the water vapor in the air. To measure the humidity, a *hygrometer* (hy-*grom*-uh-ter) is used. The word "hygrometer" is a combination of two Greek words, *hygros* ("moisture") and *metron* ("measure"). One type of hygrometer uses two thermometers. A water-soaked wick is placed on the bulb of one thermometer to keep it wet. The other thermometer is left uncovered and dry. The measurement is made by fanning both bulbs. The fanning causes the water in the wick to evaporate, thereby lowering the temperature of the wet-bulb thermometer. The temperature of the dry-bulb thermometer is not affected because no evaporation occurs. If the air is completely dry, the greatest amount of evaporation can take place. As a result, the difference between the dry-bulb reading and the wet-bulb reading is greatest. However, if the air is already full of water vapor, no further evaporation can occur. Then the dry-bulb and wet-bulb temperatures remain the same. In the first case, when the thermometers show the greatest difference, the *relative humidity* is zero. In the second case, when the thermometers are the same, it is 100 percent. When the air holds only half the water vapor that it can hold at a certain temperature, the relative humidity is 50 percent.

HYGROMETER

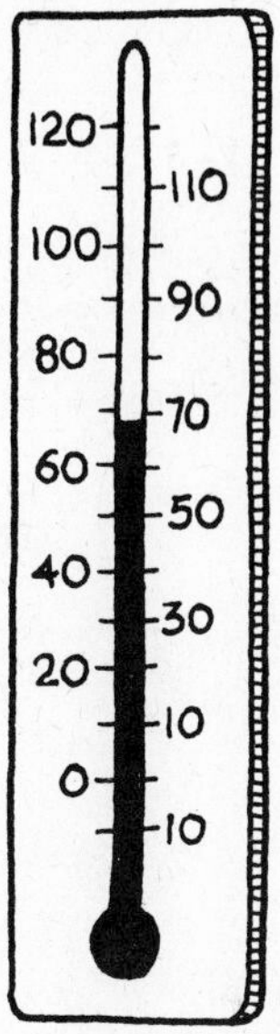

DRY BULB THERMOMETER

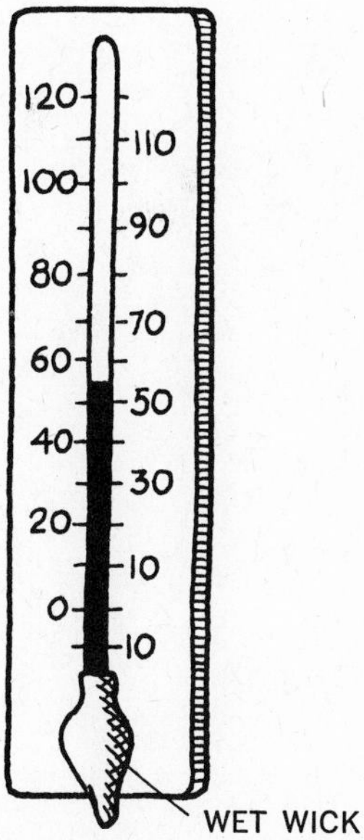

WET BULB THERMOMETER

To determine the relative humidity, take the dry-bulb reading; then take the lowest wet-bulb reading and find the difference between the two. Next use the following table. In the column at the left, find the number representing the dry reading. Move across to the column headed by the number of degrees difference. Where these two columns cross, you find the percentage of relative humidity of the air. For example, if the readings are Dry 68° F., Wet 55° F., the difference between them is 13 degrees and the relative humidity is 42 percent.

The extent to which people feel discomfort in the summertime depends upon the combined impact of temperature and humidity. From the wet- and dry-bulb reading you

HUMIDITY TABLE

Difference Between Dry-Bulb and Wet-Bulb Readings

DRY-BULB READING	1°	2°	3°	4°	5°	6°	7°	8°	9°	10°	11°	12°	13°	14°
100	96	93	89	86	83	80	77	73	70	68	65	62	59	56
98	96	93	89	86	83	79	76	73	70	67	64	61	58	56
96	96	93	89	86	82	79	76	73	69	66	63	61	58	55
94	96	93	89	85	82	79	75	72	69	66	63	60	57	54
92	96	92	89	85	82	78	75	72	68	65	62	59	56	53
90	96	92	89	85	81	78	74	71	68	65	61	58	55	52
88	96	92	88	85	81	77	74	70	67	64	61	57	54	51
86	96	92	88	84	81	77	73	70	66	63	60	57	53	50
84	96	92	88	84	80	76	73	69	66	62	59	56	52	49
82	96	92	88	84	80	76	72	69	65	61	58	55	51	48
80	96	91	87	83	79	75	72	68	64	61	57	54	50	47
78	96	91	87	83	79	75	71	67	63	60	56	53	49	46
76	96	91	87	82	78	74	70	66	62	59	55	51	48	44
74	95	91	86	82	78	74	69	65	61	58	54	50	47	43
72	95	91	86	82	77	73	69	65	61	57	53	49	45	42
70	95	90	86	81	77	72	68	64	59	55	51	48	44	40
68	95	90	85	80	76	71	67	62	58	54	50	46	42	38
66	95	90	85	80	75	71	66	61	57	53	48	44	40	36
64	95	90	84	79	74	70	65	60	56	51	47	43	38	34
62	94	89	84	79	74	69	64	59	54	50	45	41	36	32
60	94	89	83	78	73	68	63	58	53	48	43	39	34	30
58	94	88	83	77	72	66	61	56	51	46	41	37	32	27
56	94	88	82	76	71	65	60	55	50	44	39	34	30	25
54	94	88	82	76	70	64	59	53	48	42	37	32	27	22
52	94	87	81	75	69	63	57	51	46	40	35	29	24	19
50	93	87	80	74	67	61	55	49	43	38	32	27	21	16
48	93	86	79	73	66	60	54	47	41	35	29	23	18	12
46	93	86	79	72	65	58	52	45	39	32	26	20	14	8
44	93	85	78	71	63	56	49	43	36	30	23	16	10	4
42	92	85	77	69	62	55	47	40	33	26	19	12	5	
40	92	83	75	68	60	52	45	37	29	22	15	7	0	

RELATIVE HUMIDITY

can figure out the discomfort index, also known as the *temperature-humidity index* (THI). Here is the calculation:

1. Add the wet-bulb reading to the dry-bulb reading.
2. Multiply the sum by four-tenths (.4).
3. Add 15 to the result.

When the THI is over 75, more than half the people will feel discomfort. When the THI goes to 80 and higher, nearly everyone will feel discomfort.

There are some hygrometers that give a direct reading of humidity. These usually contain a clean human hair that is connected to a pointer through a system of levers. When the humidity is high, the hair stretches and the pointer moves to the higher numbers on a dial. When the humidity is low, the hair shrinks and moves the pointer toward the lower numbers.

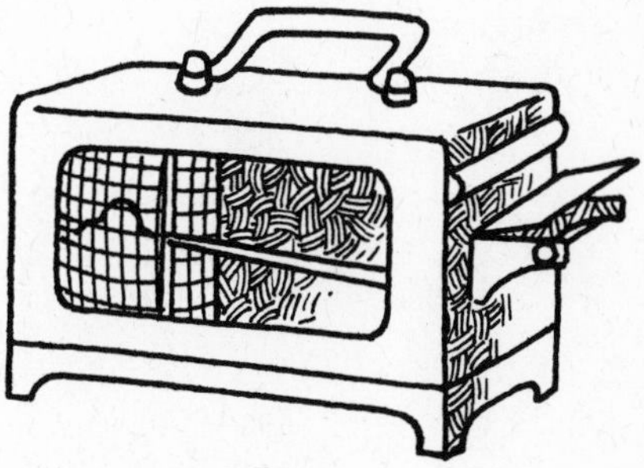

SELF-RECORDING HYGROMETER

Like the thermograph, this instrument also can be made self-recording. The same type of revolving drum is used. The recording pen is attached to a bundle of hairs, and moves up and down on the paper as the humidity changes. In this way, a continuous record of relative humidity can be made for a day or even a week.

You may have seen another simple moisture-indicating device called the *hygroscope* (*hy*-gruh-skohp). Although it does not measure the relative humidity, it does show when the air is very moist or dry. It is made by dipping a piece of paper or cloth into a solution of cobalt chloride. When the material dries, the chemical coating is blue. When the material absorbs moisture from the air, the chemical turns pink.

Even ordinary table salt gives an indication of humidity. When the humidity is high, the salt absorbs water from the air, becomes sticky and does not come out of the shaker easily.

Limestone rock also absorbs water vapor from the air. The Greek people of ancient times who lived near the Black Sea knew about this. They obtained their drinking water from chunks of limestone heaped in great piles on hills along the sea coast. During the night the rocks would soak up water from the moist sea winds that blew through them. Early next morning, fresh water was collected from the dripping-wet rocks.

Measuring Air Pressure

A most important clue to the state of the atmosphere is the pressure that air exerts. In any one place (where altitude remains the same) changes in pressure are due almost entirely to variations in the temperature and humidity of the air. High pressure is the trademark of cold, dry air, while low pressure is the mark of hot, moist air. Because of this, the air pressure in a region rises most when cold, dry air moves in, and it falls most when the air moving in is hot and moist.

We do not feel slight increases or decreases of pressure as easily as we feel changes in temperature and humidity. However, our ears are sensitive to sudden changes in pressure. When a skyscraper elevator lifts you rapidly to a high floor, where air pressure is lower than at street level, your eardrums seem to pop out. This happens because for a short time the pressure inside your body is greater than the outside pressure. On the trip down the reverse occurs, and your eardrums are pushed in. In either case, you can help balance the inner and outer pressures, to relieve the sensation in your ears, by opening your mouth or swallowing. Aside from this effect upon our ears, we have no way of detecting pressure changes except with instruments.

For the measurement of atmospheric pressure we use

a *barometer,* an instrument that was first constructed more than three hundred years ago by an Italian physicist named Torricelli (tor-uh-*chel*-ee), who was a pupil of Galileo. Torricelli poured mercury into a long glass tube that was closed at one end. Then, holding back the mercury with a finger, he turned the tube upside down and put the open end into a dish containing more mercury.

As he expected, the mercury did not pour out of the tube. Instead, its level dropped slightly and came to rest about thirty inches above the surface of the mercury in the dish. Torricelli correctly explained that the air pushing against the mercury in the dish prevented the mercury in the tube from running out. In other words, the mercury stopped moving down when the pressure due to its weight was just balanced by the pressure of the atmosphere.

TORRICELLI'S BAROMETER

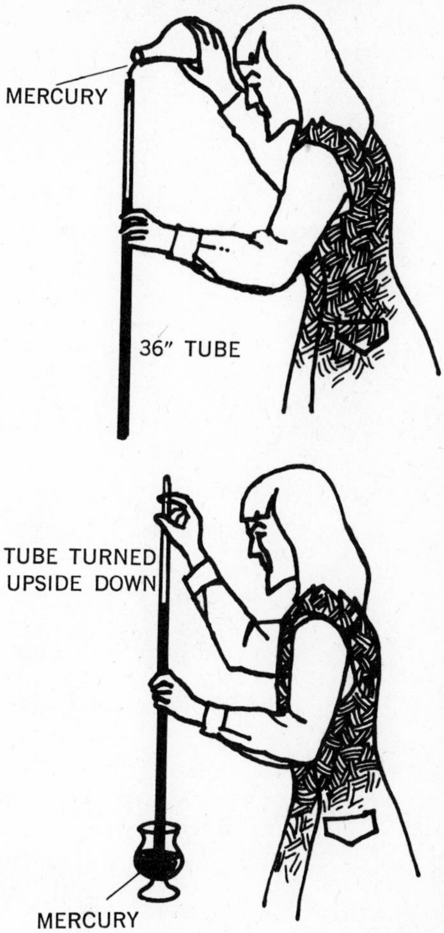

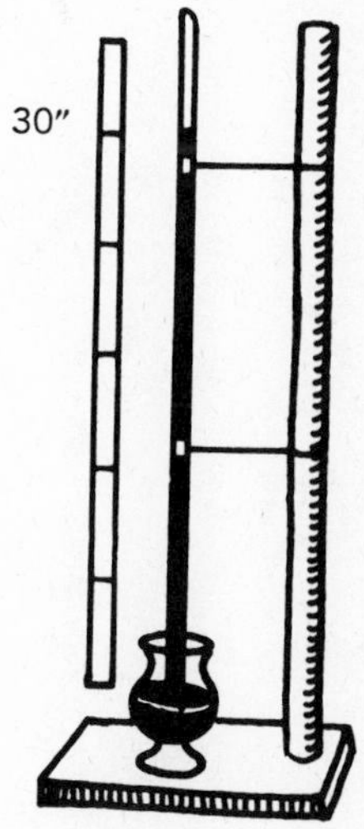

Torricelli's tube was the forerunner of the modern *mercury barometer* (buh-*rom*-uh-ter) shown on page 50. As you may have guessed, the word "barometer" combines "baros," from the Greek word for weight, with "meter." The scale of this instrument is marked so that the height of the mercury column can be measured accurately to the nearest hundredth of an inch.

At sea level, the mercury in a barometer normally stands 30 inches high. An increase in air pressure sends the mercury above the 30 mark. A decrease drops it below the 30-inch level. Air pressure is expressed in the number of *inches of mercury* that it supports. However, the Weather Bureau prefers to use the more convenient measuring unit, the *millibar* (*mil*-ih-bar). A pressure of 30 inches is equal to 1,016 millibars. To change from inches to millibars, multiply the pressure in inches by 33.87.

If you have a barometer at home or if your class has one, it probably looks like the one shown on page 50. This is an *aneroid* (*an*-er-oid) barometer. Unlike the mercury type, it contains no liquid. Instead, it has a flat metal

MERCURY BAROMETER

ANEROID BAROMETER

container from which most of the air has been removed. An increase in air pressure forces the flexible top to cave in a little. It springs out again as the pressure drops. Through a system of chains and levers, every slight movement of the top shows up as a much larger movement of the pointer on the face of the instrument.

Look closely at the scale of the aneroid barometer. Notice that the space between any two numbers, such as 29 and 30, is divided into ten parts. Each of these large divisions stands for a tenth of an inch. Each tenth, in turn, is divided into five smaller parts. This means that each subdivision represents one-fiftieth or two-hundredths of an inch. What reading is indicated by the pointer in the picture? Since the pointer is between twenty-nine and thirty, the major figure is twenty-nine. Since it is also between a small eight and a small nine, add eight-tenths. Finally, since the pointer is on three subdivisions past small eight, add six hundredths. The complete reading therefore is 29.86 inches.

The aneroid barometer has another pointer that moves only when you turn a knob that is located outside the instrument at the center of the glass face. Let us see how this pointer is used. Suppose the pressure reading is 30.20 inches at 10 A.M. You turn the movable pointer to 30.20. If at 4 P.M. the barometer reads 30.26, you know at a glance that the air pressure has gone up .06 of an inch in six hours. It is also easy to see whether the pressure has dropped or remained steady.

On the face of the dial appear the words stormy, rain, change, fair and very dry. These words should not be taken too seriously. It is the direction and the speed with which the pointer moves one way or the other, rather than the word it points to, that foretells the weather. Usually a rising barometer indicates the approach of cooler, dryer air. On the other hand, a falling barometer usually shows that warmer, moist air is moving in. A change in pressure of .1 of an inch or more in six hours is considered rapid and means a fast change in the weather.

The aneroid barometer is very compact and has nothing in it that can spill. It is good for home or school use. However, the Weather Bureau prefers the mercury barometer because for its purposes this type of instrument is more accurate.

To keep a continuous record of pressures, a *barograph* (*bar*-uh-graf) is used. Like the other "graph" instruments, it contains two basic parts. A pen moved by an aneroid mechanism writes on paper wrapped around a drum that is turned by a clock.

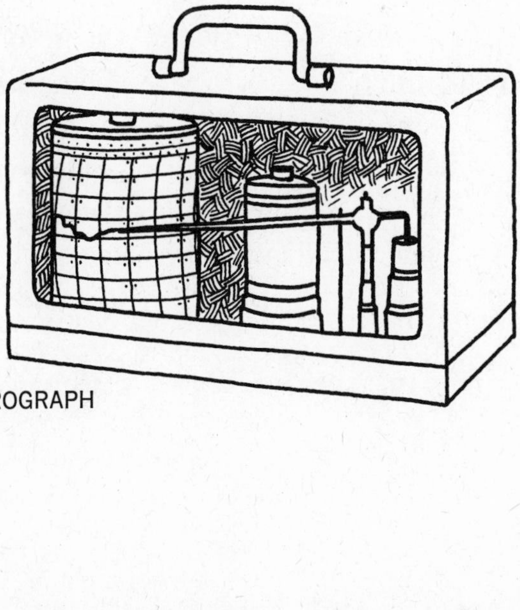

BAROGRAPH

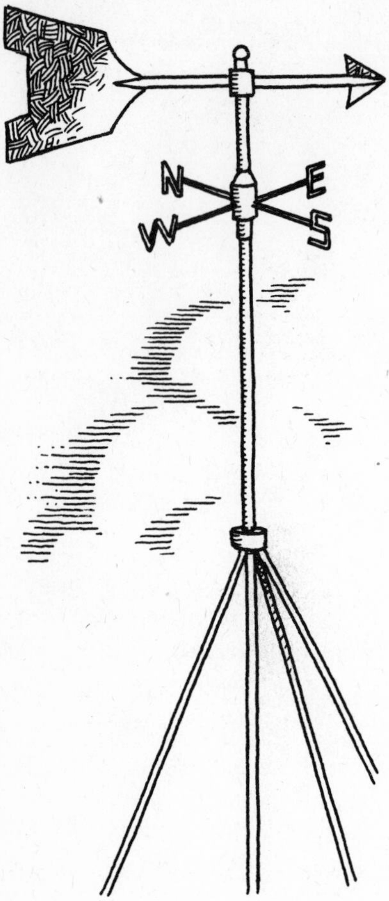

WIND VANE

Measuring Wind Speed and Direction

Every once in a while the weather remains the same for several days in a row. A stretch of time of this kind is called a "spell." It might be a hot, dry spell; a rainy spell; or a spell of fog or smog. Before such a spell ends, the winds usually change. Calm air may start moving. Gusty winds may become quiet. An east wind may shift to the west, or a north wind to the east. In other words, wind speed and direction are two additional types of clues that can help you tell in advance how the weather is going to change. To some extent you can judge the speed and direction of any wind by watching the things that it moves. A wind coming from the south would blow smoke rising out of a chimney toward the north.

Since we cannot be sure that there always will be something in sight for the wind to move, some people put up a special device for the purpose of showing wind direction. This is the *wind vane,* a familiar sight on barns and country homes. Of all the weather instruments, the wind vane is one of the simplest and probably the oldest. In the days long before scientific weather forecasting, people knew that, generally speaking, east winds meant rain; west winds, clearing; north winds, cold; and south winds, heat. From this you can see why the wind vane used to be called a weather vane.

How is a wind vane made? A figure of some kind, perhaps a rooster, a ship or even a simple arrow, is pivoted so that it swings around freely in all directions. It is balanced so that it remains level. Under the vane, there are four large letters, each representing and pointing toward one of the main directions of the compass. The arms carrying these letters are permanently attached so that they do not move.

The vane must be designed so that on one side of the

pivot a large surface is presented to the wind. On the side that points the direction, the surface is small. In the case of the arrow, the tail would be large and the head small. Any wind that blows will exert more force against the big surface and will swing the vane so that it points toward the direction from which the wind is coming. For example, if the vane points to N, the wind is coming from the north and is called a north wind. The same is true for all the other directions. In a weather station, you can see the direction of the wind by watching blinking lights or a pointer on an instrument panel. The instrument is connected electrically to the wind vane mounted high on the roof of the station. As a result, every movement of the vane is indicated immediately by the pointer or by the lights. Another type of wind direction indicator is a wind sock, which fills with air and flies with the wind.

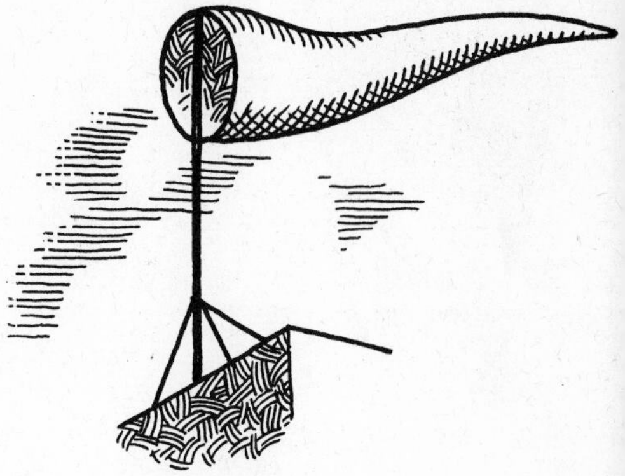

WIND SOCK

A Wind Chart has been developed to help judge the speed of the wind by its effect upon trees and smoke. Notice that in each range of speed the wind is given a particular name that helps identify it.

WIND CHART

How fast does it blow in miles per hour?	What is it called?	How does it show itself?
0	No wind (calm)	Smoke moves up straight. Flag does not fly.
1 to 4	Slight wind	Wind pushes smoke slightly away from straight line.
5 to 8	Light breeze	Face feels wind. Leaves tremble.
9 to 14	Gentle breeze	Leaves flutter steadily. Flag begins to fly.
15 to 20	Moderate wind	Small branches move. Dust is lifted and blown about.
21 to 25	Fresh wind	Small trees with leaves begin to move.
26 to 31	Strong wind	Large branches move. Wires whistle.
32 to 37	High wind	Large trees begin to sway. The wind pushes you.
38 to 43	Gale	Small branches snap off trees. The wind begins to lift you.
44 to 49	Strong gale	Larger branches snap off trees.
50 to 54	Very strong gale	Largest branches snap off trees.
55 to 60	Whole gale	Whole trees are snapped and uprooted.
61 to 66	Storm	Buildings are damaged if unprotected.
67 to 71	Violent storm	Buildings are severely damaged if unprotected.
72 to 77	Near hurricane	Slightly less violent than hurricane.
77 and up	Hurricane	Almost everything movable or breakable in path of wind is destroyed.

On a wintry day the wind can make you feel that the temperature is lower than it actually is. Why? On a calm, cold day your body heat is retained by the blanket of air that is trapped in your clothing. You feel comfortable even though it is cold. On a windy, cold day, however, the wind replaces the warm air around you with cold air. Your body then gives up heat more easily, and you feel chilled.

The relationship between the speed of the wind and the chilling effect is called the *wind-chill factor*. Winter weather reports often give this factor. For example, you may hear an announcer say, "The temperature is 20° F. However, the wind-chill factor makes it feel like 4° F."

Here is a wind-chill factor chart for low winter temperatures.

WIND-CHILL FACTOR CHART

		Air temperature in Fahrenheit degrees					
		−20°	−10°	0°	10°	20°	30°
	0	−20	−10	0	10		30
	5	−26	−15	−5	6		27
Wind	10						
Speed	15	−58	−45	−36	−18		9
in	20	−67	−53	−39	−25		4
Miles	25	−74	−59	−44	−29		0
per	30	−79	−63	−48	−33		−2
Hour	35	−82	−67	−49	−35		−4
	40	−85	−69	−53	−37		−6

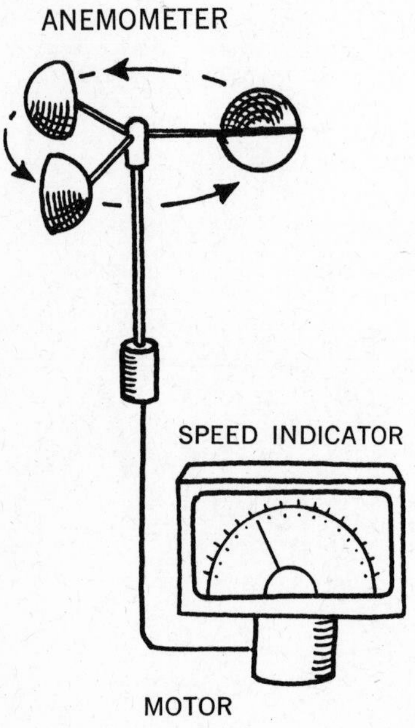

To use this chart, find the columns that show the air temperature and wind speed that are now present outside your building. Follow these columns to where they cross. The number at the intersection is the apparent temperature due to the wind-chill factor.

For exact measurement of wind speed, an instrument has to be used. Such a device is called an *anemometer* (an-uh-*mom*-uh-ter). It consists of three or four cups mounted on a rod that turns around freely. The cups catch the moving air and cause the rod to spin. The anemometer is wired to a motor that turns a pointer on the instrument panel in the weather station. The faster the wind blows, the more rapidly the rod whirls, and the higher is the speed shown by the pointer.

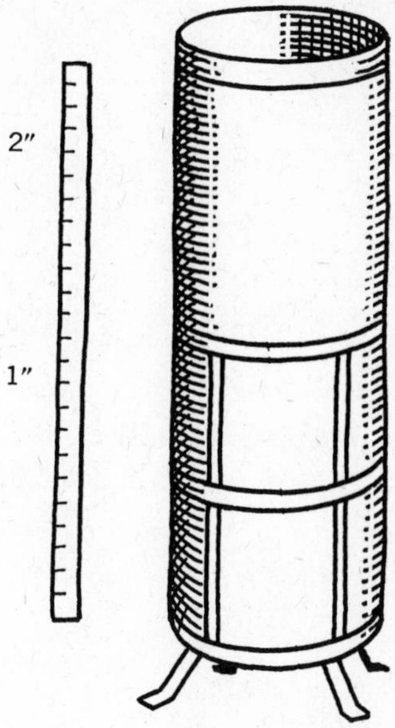

RAIN GAUGE

Measuring Rainfall and Sunshine

In this chapter, we have described some of the main tools the weatherman uses for observing and measuring weather conditions. In addition, there are two others that should be mentioned. One is the *rain gauge* (*gayj*). This is nothing more than a pan that collects rainfall in such a way as to measure the depth of the accumulated water, in inches or in fractions of inches. At the Weather Bureau a special bucket is used. It rocks back and forth each time one hundredth of an inch of rain falls into it. Each shift in its position is transmitted electrically to a counting instrument and is then automatically recorded. When the rain stops, the total fall is indicated. Ten inches of snow is equal to about one inch of rain.

The other instrument is the *sunshine recorder*. Its purpose is to register the hours of direct sunshine in a day. The record is made with the help of a little black bulb. Whenever sunlight strikes the bulb, air inside the bulb warms up and expands. An electrical switch closes, causing a recording pen in the station to draw a line on a moving piece of paper. At the end of the day, a broken line shows when and for how long the clouds blocked the sun's rays. An unbroken line means that the sun was shining all day.

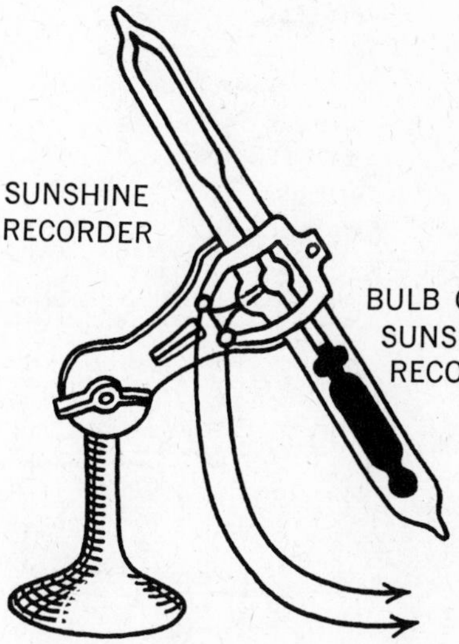

The best way to get to know the different weather instruments is to use them. Perhaps you can work with real ones at home or at school. If you cannot get the actual instrument, make your own models of them. Practice taking readings with every device that you can obtain. Practice making your own forecasts. The Weather Clue Chart gives certain clues to help you. The most important clue to remember is this—without wind, weather cannot change.

WEATHER CLUE CHART

LOOK FOR ——————————→ WHEN

	Clouds	Humidity	Pressure	Temperature	Visibility	Winds
Weather to stay FAIR	Move higher and decrease in numbers. When morning fog disappears.	Stays low	Remains steady or goes up slowly	Is normal for the season	Stays good	Are **west** to **northwest** and gentle
Weather to get WORSE	Thicken, lower and darken to the west.	Goes up	Falls steadily or rapidly	Is too high or too low for the season	Decreases	Shift to between **east** and **south**
RAIN or SNOW	Change from cirrus to lower types of rain or snow clouds.	Goes up	Falls (the faster it falls the sooner the arrival of rain or snow)	Changes rapidly	Decreases	Increase in speed, usually from the **east**
THUNDER-STORMS	Change from cumulus to cumulonimbus.	Is very high	Falls	Is very high	Decreases	Increase in speed rapidly
Weather to CLEAR	Rise and break up.	Goes down	Rises	Rises after warm front passes. Drops after cold front passes	Increases	Swing from **east** through **south** to **west**
COLDER Weather	——	Goes down	Rises	Goes down	Increases	Blow from **north** or **northwest**
WARMER Weather	——	Goes up	Falls	Goes up	Decreases	Blow from the **south**

REMEMBER ALSO:

The more of these changes you observe, the more likely the weather will be as shown above.
In some localities (West coast, Gulf coast) some of these points may not apply.
Other signs of FAIR weather are: DEW or FROST on the ground at night or early morning.
A brilliant MOON against a clear sky. A red SUNSET in a blue sky. Clearing skies.
Other signs of BAD weather are: The approach of warm, cold, or accelerated fronts as shown on weather maps.
A *RAPID* rise or drop in temperature. Darkening skies.
Unless the air over your locality moves, weather remains the same. In other words, WITHOUT WIND, WEATHER CANNOT CHANGE.

AFTER YOU MAKE YOUR FORECAST, YOU MIGHT LIKE TO ANNOUNCE IT WITH THESE WEATHER FLAGS

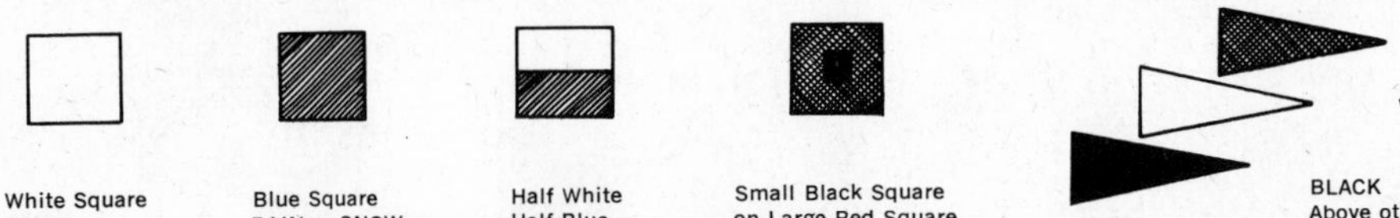

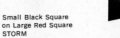

RED—East wind
WHITE—West wind

White Square
FAIR

Blue Square
RAIN or SNOW

Half White
Half Blue
SHOWERS

Small Black Square
on Large Red Square
STORM

BLACK
Above other squares—WARMER
Below other squares—COLDER

Tell your friends and neighbors about this code. If you want to fly these flags make them out of old white sheets. Use vegetable dyes for the different colors. If you want to show them in your window, use colored construction paper.

7. Uncle Sam the Weatherman

If you could observe the state of the weather around the earth every hour or two, what do you think you would see? Somewhere or other you most certainly would spot such weather conditions as raging blizzards, tropical rainstorms, swirling hurricanes, sandstorms, funnel-shaped tornadoes, electrical storms, patches of cloudless skies, earth-shrouding fog and storms at sea. The circulation of the atmosphere carries these conditions from place to place around the earth. Your overall view would enable you to chart the paths of these events and the speeds with which they travel. You could broadcast this information to the people on earth to give them advance notice of the weather that is moving into any particular area. Although manned weather observation stations do not yet orbit the earth, we are making steady progress in that direction. No matter how observations are made in the future, we will continue to rely on the reports of the Weather Bureau. Here is the story of how this Bureau was formed and how it does its work.

Before rapid communication systems were developed, local weather observers were almost completely isolated from one another. If one in California tried to send information by pony express to another in Ohio, the weather from the west might reach the east before the message got there. It was not until different parts of the country were linked by telegraph that people had the first practical means of sending information about weather conditions across the country. As the telegraph network grew, it became possible to set up a national weather service. This was done by an act of Congress in 1870. By this act, the service was authorized to prepare storm and flood warnings, and keep a file of weather records. The Weather Bureau itself was established in 1890.

THEODOLITE

In the years that followed, tremendous progress was made in the means of communication. In rapid succession the telephone, teletype, radio, *facsimile* (fak-*sim*-ih-lee) system for sending pictures, and television helped speed up the exchange of reports. Also as a result of this, it became possible to set up more stations at widely scattered locations.

At the present time, the main office of the United States Weather Bureau, located in Washington, D.C., receives messages from thousands of observation centers. These come from about 600 places within the United States itself; from 150 other points in North America; from some 150 ships in the northern waters of the Atlantic and Pacific Oceans; and from nearly 2,000 foreign stations in South America, Europe, Asia and Africa.

Centers in the United States report weather conditions over their part of the earth's surface at least four times a day. This information is entered on weather maps and is sent by facsimile transmission from the national center to many regional offices. For sixty cents a month, you can receive each day a copy of the official Weather Bureau map for 1:00 A.M. Eastern Standard Time. Send a check or money order for that amount to the Superintendent of Documents, Washington, D.C. 20402.

In the search for facts, many of the Bureau's stations use special devices to explore the upper levels of the atmosphere. You can get some information about wind high up in the air just by flying a kite. When it is aloft, it sails in the direction toward which the wind blows. The pull on the kite string gives you an indication of the force and speed of the wind. If you have ever let go of a helium-filled balloon and sadly watched it disappear, you know that it too revealed the direction and speed of the air currents that carried it away.

It should not surprise you to learn that balloons are deliberately released at some one hundred fifty observation points, four times a day. They are filled with just the right amount of helium or hydrogen to make them go up at a definite speed. At night the balloon carries a flashlight. From the ground, the movement of each pilot balloon is followed with a small telescope. The height of the balloon is figured from the angle at which the telescope is tilted. A telescope mounted for this purpose is called a *theodolite* (thee-*od*-oh-lite).

Another type of balloon is set loose twice a day from about sixty stations. These do not have to be tracked by visual means. A *radiosonde* (*ray*-dee-oh-sond) is suspended from each balloon. In it, special instruments are hooked up to a tiny radio transmitter. Changes in temperature, pressure and humidity are translated into electrical signals, which then are broadcast to earth by the radio. The signals are received at the station and are translated back into ordinary measurements. After the balloon

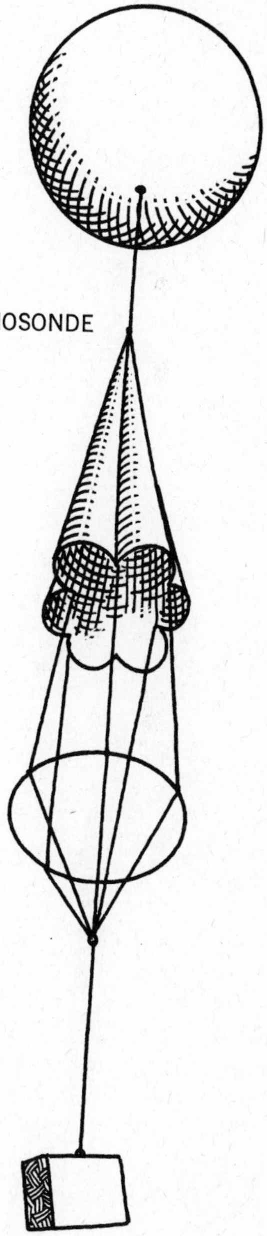
RADIOSONDE

reaches a certain altitude, it breaks and a parachute opens to return the radiosonde to the earth. If you ever find one, return it by mail according to instructions on the box. With the help of this device, atmospheric conditions have been explored up to a height of about twenty miles.

One result of such exploration was the discovery of *jet streams*. Jet streams are currents of air that flow in winding paths at altitudes between 10,000 and 40,000 feet. Some jet streams travel at speeds as high as 300 miles per hour, usually moving from west to east. Jet streams exert great influence on the transportation of huge quantities of air from one place to another. As a result, the shifting streams bring changes in the weather.

During World War II, special radio waves were used to detect the approach of enemy aircraft and to find out how far away they were. The equipment used to broadcast and receive such waves is called *radar* (*ray*-dahr), from the contraction of the technical phrase "*ra*dio *d*etection *a*nd *r*anging." In the manner of a searchlight, a radar transmitter sends out a beam of invisible radio waves. Objects in the path of the beam reflect some of the waves. When these bounce back to the unit, the shapes of the objects show up on a radar scope, which is like the picture tube of a television set. Although radar was used mainly for military purposes at first, it was not long before the radar operators noticed that clouds, rain and snow also reflected the radar waves and showed up on the screen. Now, many weather stations are equipped with radar to search the skies for cloud formations too far away to be seen with the eye.

Years ago, the New York City office of the Weather Bureau installed a new radar unit. According to the weatherman in charge of the office, the unit can locate storms as far away as 200 miles. When storm clouds appear on the scope, their distance, altitude and speed of approach can be figured out. If a violent storm is discovered to be 180 miles away and moving toward New York City at 20 miles per hour, the Bureau can warn of its approach about nine hours before it actually arrives. Here are two pictures of new equipment. In one you see how a cloud formation shows up on the two radar scopes. The other shows a view of the plastic dome that protects the antenna.

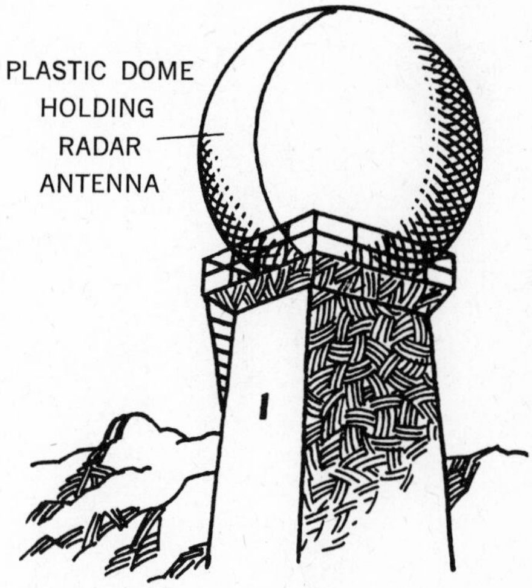

Storms that start many hundreds of miles out at sea cannot yet be discovered by land-based radar. One such storm, the hurricane, usually begins over tropical ocean waters. When the Weather Bureau learns that a hurricane is forming, the stations located on the east coast of the United States swing into action. They ask the ships at sea to radio reports of local conditions every hour or so. Radiosonde and ground observations are made more frequently.

But the menace of a hurricane is so great that information about it must be obtained even faster than is possible with the usual methods. To meet this kind of emergency, Air Force and Navy reconnaissance airplanes are equipped as flying weather stations. Daring pilots fly the planes

right into the heart of the storm and all around it. They make every necessary measurement and radio the results to the mainland. From these reports the Weather Bureau can pinpoint the position of the storm and keep accurate track of its direction and speed. Thanks to the "hurricane hunters," who ride the fury of the storm, people in its path are warned far enough in advance to be able to take the proper steps to safeguard life and property.

The development of high-powered rockets has given us still another method of hunting for clues to future weather—the use of photography to analyze cloud formations. This photograph taken from the Apollo 10 spacecraft shows a view of the earth from 250,000 miles away. The west coast of North American can be seen through the cloud cover.

So far, in this chapter, we have described some of the ways of collecting weather facts from thousands of ground stations and hundreds of hard-to-reach parts of the atmosphere. If this information arrived as plain words at central headquarters where the forecasters work, it would be impossible to handle all the paper carrying the messages. How would you get around this difficulty? You would make up a code, of course. This is just what was done by weathermen all over the world. They agreed to use certain numbers and symbols to stand for different weather conditions. You can travel to any country, walk into a weather station and find charts of this code. Although the numbers and symbols would be the same everywhere, their meanings would in each case be given in the language of the country. Weathermen have an international language.

Here is a sample of a coded message as it might appear on the tape coming out of a teletype machine.

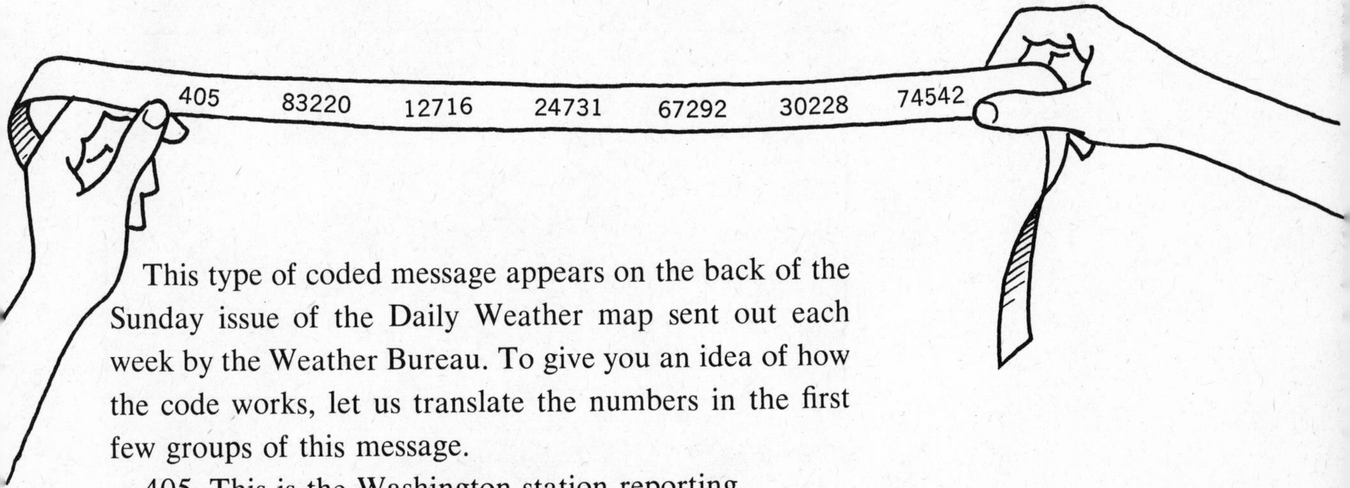

This type of coded message appears on the back of the Sunday issue of the Daily Weather map sent out each week by the Weather Bureau. To give you an idea of how the code works, let us translate the numbers in the first few groups of this message.

405 This is the Washington station reporting.
8 The sky is completely covered with clouds.
32 A northwest wind is blowing.
20 Its speed is 20 knots (23 miles per hour).
12 Visibility is 12/16 of a mile.
71 At present a slight snow is falling steadily.
6 Just before the snow, it was raining.
247 Air pressure is 1024.7 millibars.
31 Air temperature is 31° F.

The remaining numbers indicate the types of clouds at different levels, the time at which precipitation started, how many inches fell, which way and how fast the pressure is changing and several other facts. It is amazing that so much can be told with only thirty-three numbers.

How do weathermen bring together these messages from hundreds and hundreds of places, in a form that can give a complete picture of conditions all over the country? First, they take each report and compress it still further into a small cluster of symbols and numbers arranged according to a certain pattern. In this cluster, most items that are actual measurements appear as numbers. Others, of a descriptive nature, such as cloud types, are represented by symbols. The sample message we have been using would look like this.

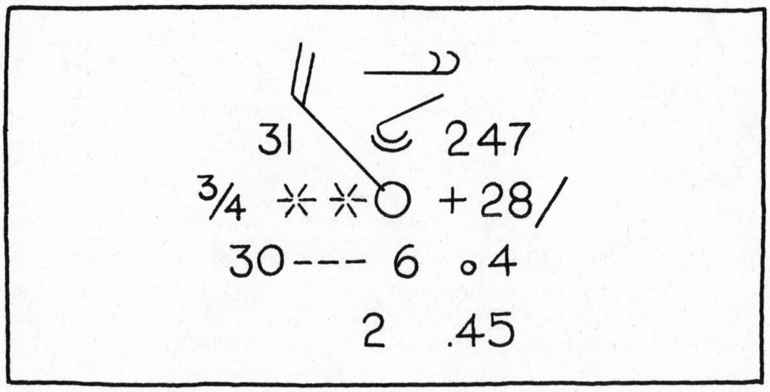

The cluster is called a *station model.*

The next step is to put the model for each reporting station in its geographic position on a large map of the United States. When this is done, the map gives a "bird's-eye" view of the weather picture for the country. To make the picture more meaningful, lines are drawn connecting all places reporting the same pressure. Such lines are called *isobars* (*eye*-soh-barz), a word meaning equal pressure. From these isobars, it is easy to see where the regions of *high* and *low pressures* (highs and lows) are located. Areas of precipitation are shaded. On the map, special lines called *fronts* are drawn to show the boundary between two different bodies of air. Cold air is steadily trying to push down from the north. Warm air from the south tries to move the opposite way. These bodies of air often come into conflict. When the cold air advances against the warm, the line along which this occurs is called a *cold front*. It is shown on the map like this—  . When the warm air is doing the pushing, the line is called a *warm front* and is pictured this way—  . A boundary line that does not move one way or the other, is called a *stationary front*. It is represented by this symbol—  . When cold air on each side of warm air lifts it up from the ground level, this forms an *occluded* (ok-*kloo*-dead) *front,* indicated

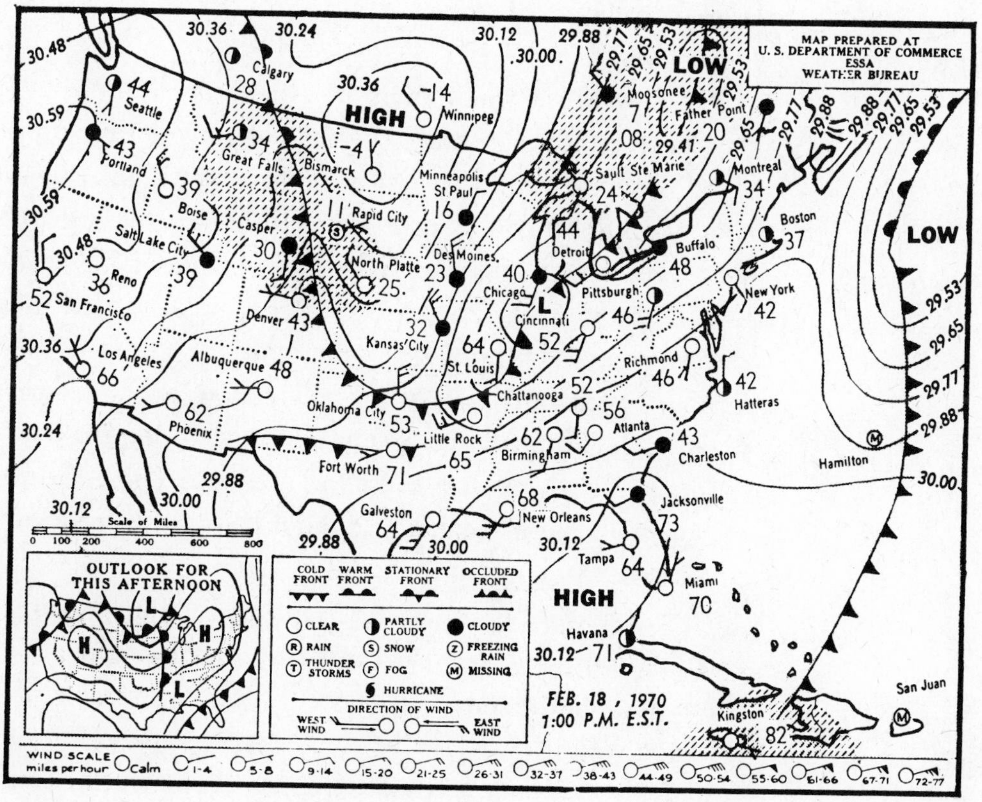

like this—  . The fronts that appear on a map are very important clues because each is accompanied by its own special pattern of clouds and weather.

The completed map is put on a facsimile transmitter and is sent to major points throughout the United States several times a day. At the local station receiving the maps, the forecaster gets a good idea of the trend of the weather for his locality. He compares the latest map with previous ones. He sees what fronts and pressure areas are approaching. He knows that highs and lows generally move eastward at a speed of about 500 miles a day in the summertime and about 700 miles a day in the winter. Highs usually bring fair weather, and lows usually bring rain or snow. By combining the information he gets from the map with the local changes shown by his own instruments, he has a basis for making a good prediction. Actually such predictions are correct about 85 percent of the time.

When weather conditions threaten lives or property, the Weather Bureau issues special bulletins. These may warn of approaching hurricanes, tornadoes, blizzards, flood conditions, frost danger, extreme cold or heat waves. You can see how important it is for a community to have this information in time to take action to safeguard life and property.

When winds dangerous to navigation are forecast, warning flags are hoisted at coastal areas during the day. At night, light signals are used. The above chart shows the arrangement of pennants and lights for different wind conditions.

As an aid to air traffic, the Weather Bureau prepares and distributes daily weather maps showing upper air winds and temperatures. In 1959, to keep up with the jet age, the Weather Bureau began to issue maps and forecasts for altitudes between 20,000 and 40,000 feet. Seven special centers cooperate in gathering information for these high-altitude forecasts. These stations are located at Suitland, Maryland; New York International Airport; Miami, Florida; San Juan, Puerto Rico; San Francisco, California; Anchorage, Alaska; and Honolulu, Hawaii.

To help farmers, fruit growers, forest rangers, shipping lines, power companies and other groups plan their activities, the Weather Bureau prepares forecasts for longer periods of time. A five-day forecast is issued twice a week. A thirty-day forecast, called a monthly outlook, is issued at the beginning and middle of each month.

Day by day the Weather Bureau accumulates weather statistics from all parts of the country. Some 9,000 people, called cooperative observers, help complete the picture by mailing in information from isolated areas. As you become a more skilled observer you might want to join this group yourself. Apply to the Weather Bureau to find out how to do this. Each set of observations is recorded as holes punched into a card. The cards are filed at the National Weather Record Center, at Asheville, N.C. There are about 600,000,000 cards in this collection, with some 25,000,000 being added every year. With the help of modern machines that classify these cards, the Weather Bureau performs another type of service. It issues weekly, monthly and yearly summaries of past weather.

Now you have a general idea of the basic services and

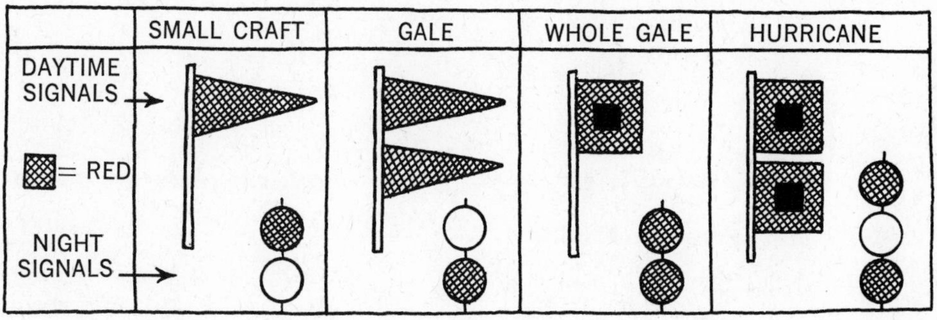

WARNING SIGNALS DISPLAYED BY U.S. WEATHER STATIONS ALONG SEACOASTS

activities of the Weather Bureau. But there is more to the story. Year after year meteorologists keep on discovering new facts that add to our understanding of the forces that shape the earth's weather. The next chapter deals with some of these discoveries. Before you begin to read about them, let us look at some of the legends that used to guide people in their effort to foretell weather, before the existence of the modern Weather Bureau service.

Here are some of the things that people used to go by. In the chart that follows, the legends are listed as Reliable, Sometimes Reliable, and Unreliable. From what you now know about weather, try to figure out why each legend is rated the way it is. Here is a hint. Plants and animals have no way of foretelling weather.

WEATHER LEGENDS

R. – Reliable; S.R. = Sometimes Reliable; U. = Unreliable

1. Rain before seven,
   Clear before eleven. (R.)
2. Evening red, morning gray
   speeds a traveler on his way. (R.)
3. Evening gray, morning red
   Brings down rain upon his head. (R.)
4. Rainbow at night, sailor's delight,
   Rainbow at morning, sailor's warning. (R.)
5. Wind in the west
   Suits everyone best. (R.)
6. Rain is near when curls disappear. (S.R.)
7. Mackerel skies and mares' tails
   Make lofty ships carry low sails. (R.)
8. Forty days of rain follow a rainy
   St. Swithin's day (Aug. 23). (U.)
9. When crickets' chirps grow loud and strong
   A storm will rage before too long. (S.R.)
10. When the moon is spilling water
    it will rain the next day. (U.)
11. When the dew is on the grass
    Rain will never come to pass. (R.)
12. A growing halo round the moon
    Tells of rain that's coming soon. (R.)
13. If woolly fleeces spread the heavenly way
    No rain be sure disturbs the summer day. (R.)
14. When the glass falls low prepare for a blow
    When it rises high let all your kites fly. (R.)
15. Wind from south, rain is in its mouth
    Smoke to west, good weather past
    Smoke to east, good weather next. (R.)
16. When the comb crackles through the hair
    Look for weather clear and fair. (R.)
17. When corns and joints begin to ache
    An umbrella be sure to take. (S.R.)
18. Woolly bear caterpillar with wide brown band
    Means a long, cold winter o'er all the land. (U.)
19. If the groundhog sees his shadow and runs right back to sleep (Feb. 2)
    Then 'tis sure for six weeks more the wintertime will keep.
    But if clouds block out his sight and he stays out for a fling
    Then by this token be assured there'll be an early spring. (U.)

8. A Forecast for Your Future

How can man become master of the weather? One way is to be able to control the weather, either by stopping it before it sets in or by changing (modifying) it after it begins. A second way is to be able to predict the weather accurately and far enough in advance so that people can arrange to protect themselves against its harmful effects.

What techniques for modifying the weather have been explored? A method was developed after Dr. Vincent Schaefer, Dr. Irving Langmuir and other scientists discovered that rain or snow could be made to fall from certain types of clouds if the clouds were sprinkled with bits of chemical materials. A way of "seeding" a cloud is to spray the chemicals from an airplane flying through it.

Another method of cloud seeding is to blow the material up from the ground. In separate trials, tiny bits of dry ice, silver iodide crystals or carbon dust have been

used for this purpose. A cloud is produced by seeding, provided that sufficient water vapor is present in the air. Researchers at the University of Arizona discovered in 1958 that clouds seeded with silver iodide produced nine times as many lightning flashes as those that were not given the chemical treatment. It is hard to tell what other strange facts such experiments will reveal.

Some years ago, the United States Navy announced that, in tests over Georgia, clouds were made to appear and disappear by seeding the air with finely powdered carbon. In one test, an airplane sprayed water containing six pounds of carbon dust along a one mile path. Soon, a cloud one mile long and three thousand feet thick began to form. In a second demonstration, seeding with carbon caused a cloud six thousand feet high to vanish in twenty minutes. To make a cloud disappear, its top is sprayed with the dust.

The harnessing of *nuclear* (*noo*-klee-ahr) *power* may give man still another weapon in his battle to control the elements. How will it be used? Let us look ahead to the twenty-first century.

Food crops will be growing in the deserts of the world. With nuclear power, rivers will be shifted and artificial lakes will be created to bring water to places that used to be the driest regions on earth. New harbors will appear in cities that had small harbors or no harbors before. Huge deposits of national resources will be discovered by penetrating more deeply into the earth. All of these things will be done with nuclear power.

Before scientists really try to make changes like those we have just imagined, they will have to be sure the projects are completely safe. Although it has been suggested that the ice caps might be melted, it would not make much sense to do this if the oceans were to rise high enough to flood the coastal cities of the world. When the time comes for such projects, scientists will have to do some very careful planning. Citizens will have to know enough science so that they may vote intelligently on whether or not to approve these projects.

What are scientists doing to increase the range and accuracy of weather predictions? With the help of new methods and devices they are seeking to find out more about solar flares and their electrical, magnetic and heating effects on earth; more about the polar regions; more about jet streams and ocean currents; more about the earth's own heat; and more about the entire atmosphere.

Rockets, man-made *satellites* (*sat*-uh-lytes), and space probes, launched in connection with the exploration of outer space, for the first time in history are putting us in touch with conditions in the very outermost limits of the atmosphere. The early satellites revealed that air particles extend farther into space and that the air is about twice as dense as we thought.

On April 1, 1960, a new era of weather observing began when the United States launched Tiros I, the first in a series of weather satellites. On its second orbit, Tiros I began to photograph the earth, clouds and storms and transmit the pictures by television to ground stations.

Weighing 270 pounds and carrying two cameras,

Tiros I was designed to take pictures for three months from a height of about 450 miles above the earth. The word Tiros comes from the first letters of the satellite's full name, Television and Infrared Observation Satellite. The cameras of Tiros I were able to take daytime pictures of the earth and clouds in ordinary visible light, and night-time pictures in the invisible infrared light given off by the warm earth and clouds. With the launching of Tiros I, an age-old dream came true. At last the weathermen had "eyes" high above the earth with which they could see the ever-changing patterns of clouds in the atmosphere and keep track of the birth, growth and movement of hurricanes, tornadoes and other storms.

In 1966 the Environmental Science Services Administration launched the Environmental Survey Satellites (ESSA) 1 and 2. These satellites were designed to photograph the clouds over small regions of the earth as well as the cloud cover all around the earth. From time to time additional ESSA satellites were launched to keep the system in operation.

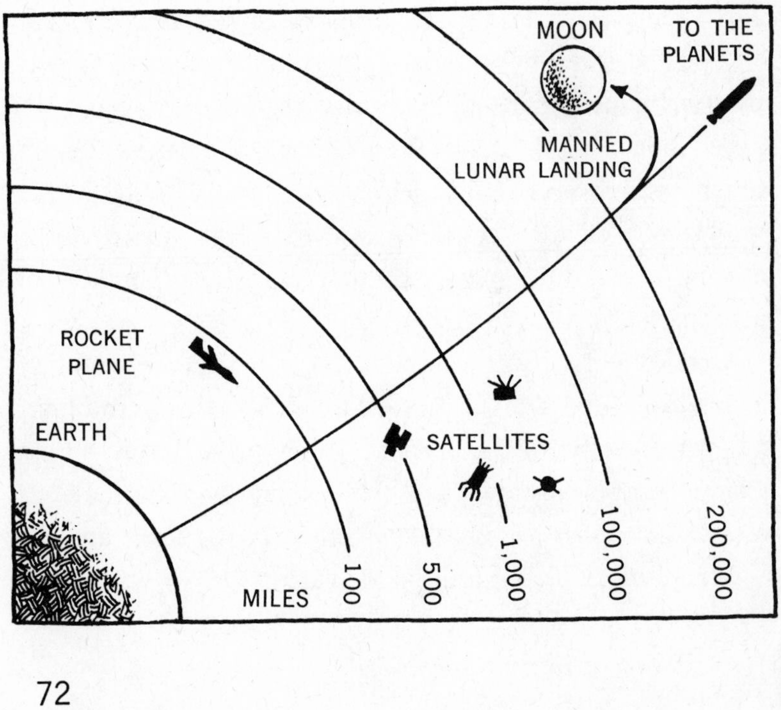

WEATHER SATELLITES

Satellite	Date of launch	Points of interest
VANGUARD 2	February 17 ,1959	Transmitted first pictures of the earth's cloud cover.
TIROS 1	April 1, 1960	First weather satellite. Took 23,000 photos of clouds.
TIROS 2	November 23, 1960	Obtained 36,000 cloud-cover photographs.
TIROS 3	July 12, 1961	Spotted growth of 50 tropical storms.
TIROS 4	February 8, 1962	Obtained over 32,500 cloud photos.
TIROS 5	June 19, 1962	Obtained 58,000 cloud photos.
TIROS 6	September 18, 1962	Obtained over 66,000 cloud photos. Spotted 13 hurricanes.
TIROS 7	June 19, 1963	Carried equipment for infrared experiments.
TIROS 8	December 21, 1963	Carried Automatic Picture Transmission (APT) system. Sent photos continuously to 400 ground stations.
TIROS 9	January 22, 1965	First weather satellite launched into polar orbit. From this orbit the entire spinning earth passes in review.
TIROS 10	July 2, 1965	Completed Tiros series.
NIMBUS 1	August 28, 1964	Specially equipped to take infrared photographs at night.
NIMBUS 2	May 15 ,1966	From polar orbit, transmitted two pictures daily of the entire earth's surface.
NIMBUS 3	April 14, 1969	Equipped with two nuclear generators to boost electric power of solar cells. First use of atomic energy in weather satellite. Equipped to measure temperature and humidity at various levels of the atmosphere under the satellite.
ATS 1	December 6, 1966	In hovering orbit 22,300 miles above equator. Every 24 minutes camera can photograph circular portion of earth with radius of more than 4,000 miles. Photos can be merged into slow-motion pictures of cloud movements and changes.
ATS 3	November 5, 1967	Same as ATS 1. ATS 2 not in operation.
ESSA 1	February 1, 1966	Launched in polar orbit. Two wide-angle cameras photograph the entire earth every day. Pictures are stored. On command they are transmitted to a special picture-receiving station on earth.
ESSA 2	February 28, 1966	Launched in polar orbit. Equipped for automatic picture transmission (APT). Cameras send pictures immediately to more than 400 receiving stations all over the world.
ESSA 3	October 2, 1966	Same as ESSA 1
ESSA 4	January 26, 1967	Same as ESSA 2
ESSA 5	April 20, 1967	Same as ESSA 1
ESSA 6	November 10, 1967	Same as ESSA 2
ESSA 7	August 16, 1968	Same as ESSA 1
ESSA 8	December 15, 1968	Same as ESSA 2
ESSA 9	February 26, 1969	Same as ESSA 1

VANGUARD II

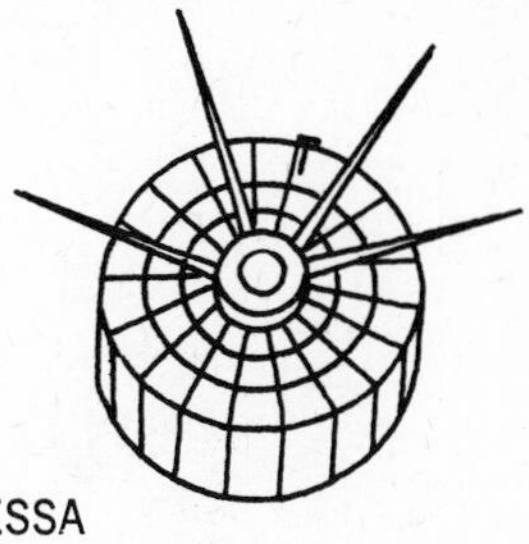
ESSA

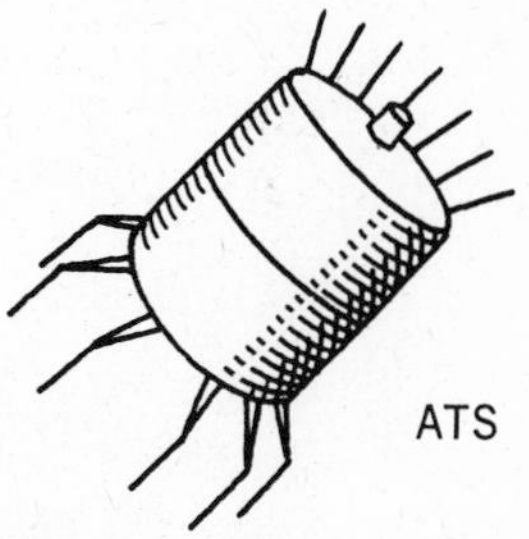
ATS

TIROS

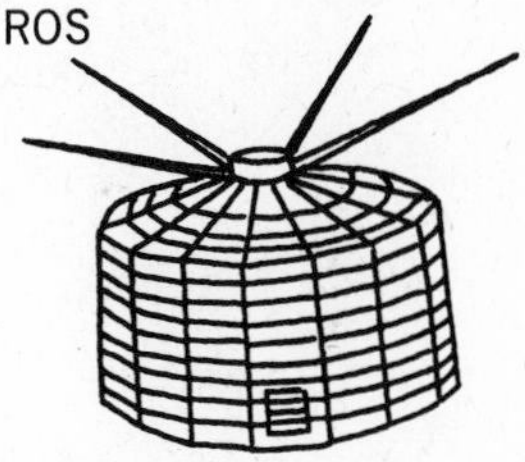

NIMBUS

Another group of satellites is known as the Nimbus series. Besides obtaining infrared and daylight pictures, the Nimbus satellites can measure from above the different temperatures and humidities of the lower levels of the atmosphere. Since ground observations cover only about 20 percent of the earth, the Nimbus satellites will help fill the 80 percent gap in information about the atmosphere.

The Applications Technology Satellite (ATS) is in a very special class. It is put into an orbit that is 22,300 miles above the earth. At that height the satellite circles the earth at the same speed as the earth rotates on its axis. As a result, the ATS remains (hovers) over the same portion of the earth and keeps on taking photographs of that region only. As additional ATS satellites are launched, we will be able to keep under constant observation, in full color, more and more sections of the earth. Eventually we will be able to see the entire face at one time.

Weather satellites transmit their pictures and measurements in rapid-fire succession. Other satellites that serve as relay stations in a worldwide communications network also speed the collection of weather data. The result is staggering. The human mind cannot put this information together quickly enough for the purpose of preparing forecasts before the weather occurs. Only the electronic computer can work at speeds rapid enough to digest the information, analyze it and come up with forecasts.

Some computers are designed to receive thousands of separate photographs and combine them into one picture that reveals basic weather systems all over the world for a particular time. Other computers are designed to receive from land stations millions of measurements of humidity, pressure, temperature, wind direction and wind speed. These computers translate this information into a weather map that shows at a glance what the weather is and, within minutes, arrive at a prediction of what the weather is likely to be the next hour, tomorrow or even next week.

As the speed of operation increases, the time should come when computers will be able to make long-range forecasts for periods of a week or more into the future. It is estimated that accurate long-range forecasting would result in annual savings of millions of dollars. Advance warning would give people enough time to protect themselves, their crops and their personal property from the destructive effects of such bad weather conditions as cold waves, drought, floods, fog, hailstorms, hot spells, hurricanes, lightning, smog, temperature inversions and tornadoes.

Our ambition to be able to make weather "to order" may be realized some day, perhaps within your own lifetime. Years from now, you may open your morning paper and find a startling headline that reads, "City Weather Selector Now in Operation." How will the selector work? Perhaps the entire city will be enclosed in a huge plastic dome. Perhaps automatic controls will provide everyone under the dome with regulated sunshine, wind, rain, humidity and plenty of unpolluted air. Use your imagination to picture other systems of weather control. What will the actual systems be? Only the future can tell.

The future also holds a great deal in store for you personally. Would you like to become a weather scientist (*meteorologist*)? Would you like to help make some of the discoveries in the years to come?

How should you prepare to do this? Start by being alert. Ask questions, get answers, practice observing, perform experiments, keep records, visit weather centers, talk to weathermen, read science books, keep up with weather news, construct measuring instruments, use your brain to figure out the how and why of things, use your imagination, think of new ways of explaining and doing things, practice the ways of the scientist.

Learn as much as you can in all subjects. Pay special attention to science and mathematics.

Make sure you elect earth science, chemistry and physics as part of your science program. Also take at least three years of mathematics. Join the school science or weather club. If there is none, start one.

In college, continue your study of science and mathematics. Elect such courses as *geology* (jee-*ol*-uh-jee) (science of the earth) and *meteorology* (mee-tee-er-*ol*-uh-jee) (science of weather). Obtain your bachelor's degree (B.S.). Later you may want to specialize still more by taking graduate work toward advanced degrees—master's degree (M.S.) and doctor's degree (Ph.D.).

After graduation from college, or even before, you may wish to take a Civil Service examination for a position as meteorologist with the Weather Bureau. If you do, get more information from the Civil Service Commission in Washington, D.C. Airlines, public utilities, television and radio stations, and private weather-forecasting agencies also employ meteorologists.

Even if you do not choose meteorology as your career, a good knowledge of science and mathematics will help you understand the world of tomorrow and get a good job.

If you do become a weather scientist, or any other kind of a scientist, you may have a big part in *shaping* the world of tomorrow.

for further reading

ADLER, IRVING. *Dust.* New York: The John Day Company, 1958.

BELL, THELMA H. *Snow.* New York: The Viking Press, 1954.

BENDICK, JEANNE. *Lightning.* Chicago: Rand McNally, 1961.

CARLSON, C. W. and B. W. *Water Fit To Use.* New York: The John Day Company, 1966.

EPSTEIN, SAM and BERYL. *All About the Desert.* New York: Random House, 1957.

FENTON, CARROLL and MILDRED. *Our Changing Weather.* New York: Doubleday and Company, 1954.

FISHER, R. M. *How To Know and Predict the Weather.* New York: The New American Library, 1953.

FORRESTER, FRANK H. *Thousand and One Questions Answered About the Weather.* New York: Dodd, Mead and Co., 1957.

IRVING, ROBERT. *Hurricanes and Glaciers.* New York: Random House, 1955.

KAVALER, LUCY. *Dangerous Air.* New York: The John Day Company, 1967.

KNIGHT, DAVID C. *Science Book of Meteorology.* New York: Franklin Watts, 1964.

LEHR, P. E., BURNETT, R. W. and ZIM, H. S. *Weather.* New York: Simon and Schuster, 1957.

MILGROM, HARRY. *Explorations in Science.* New York: E. P. Dutton and Company, 1961.

———. *First Experiments with Gravity.* New York: E. P. Dutton and Company, 1966.

———. *Further Explorations in Science.* New York: E. P. Dutton and Company, 1963.

MUELLER, ROBERT E. *Eyes in Space.* New York: The John Day Company, 1965.

NORLING, JO and ERNEST. *First Book of Water.* New York: Franklin Watts, 1952.

SPILHAUS, ATHELSTAN. *Satellite of the Sun.* New York: The Viking Press, 1958.

STAMBLER, IRWIN. *Weather Instruments: How They Work.* New York: G. P. Putnam's Sons, 1968.

TANNEHILL, IVAN R. *All About the Weather.* New York: Random House, 1953.

WINCHESTER, JAMES H. *Hurricanes, Storms, Tornadoes.* New York: G. P. Putnam's Sons, 1968.

WISE, WILLIAM. *Killer Smog.* Chicago: Rand McNally, 1968.

WYLER, ROSE. *First Book of Weather.* New York: Franklin Watts, 1956.

WYLER, ROSE and AMES, GERALD. *The Story of the Ice Age.* New York: Harper and Brothers, 1956.

ZIM, HERBERT S. *Lightning and Thunder.* New York: William Morrow and Co., 1954.

Weather Bureau Publications. Superintendent of Documents, Washington, D.C. 20402.

Atmospheric Sciences	$ .20
Clouds	$ .25
Hurricane Information and Atlantic Tracking Chart	$ .15
Lightning	$ .15
Thunderstorms	$ .15
Tornado	$ .20
Weather Maps, weekly series	$4.50
Weather Publications, Price List 48	*Free*

index